DUNKIRK
of a very young soldier

To the "girl-friend" of this story – since 1946, my wife

This revised and expanded edition of the Dunkirk Diary has been prepared by the widow and two sons of Wilf Saunders as a tribute to their Father and to widen awareness of the events surrounding Dunkirk for the Seventieth Anniversary.

DUNKIRK DIARY
of a very young soldier

Wilf Saunders CBE

BREWIN BOOKS

First published by
Birmingham Public Libraries, 1989

This edition published by
Brewin Books Ltd, 56 Alcester Road,
Studley, Warwickshire, B80 7LG in 2010

www.brewinbooks.com

ISBN: 978-1-85858-461-4

A Cataloguing in Publication Record
for this title is available from the British Library.

Typeset in Baskerville
Printed in Great Britain by
Information Press Ltd.

CONTENTS

FOREWORD

Playing a real life character is a challenge, but one which brings many rewards.

For me, reading about Wilf's experiences at Dunkirk was an education. Not only through my learning about places, dates and events during that period of history, but also understanding how these events affected the man emotionally and appreciating more deeply how he contended with them. In his diaries, Wilf can teach us great lessons about dignity, humility and finding strength in the face of adversity.

I was entranced by the diaries and became devoted to them during filming – they became my bible. He writes so clearly and passionately and makes you participate in these remarkable events, enabling the reader to fully realise his experiences, good and bad.

When we filmed in Dunkirk, on the actual beach where the soldiers were evacuated, it was easy to get carried away with the emotion of the recreation – the evocative nature of what we were shooting. As an actor I found it impossible not to feel the loss, the pain and the futility of what happened on those beaches. But for Wilf "Survival was key" and in character that became my mantra.

These diaries are important and symbolic. They symbolise something very important about pain, suffering and the power of the human spirit to overcome catastrophe.

Apparently, to understand the human condition properly you have to be pained by human experience. But far from making us feel empty about the world, Wilf Saunders gives us great hope.

Michael Legge

PREFACE

The germ of the idea which led to the writing of this small book is to be found in my decision to keep a daily journal during my service with the B.E.F. in France, from early January to the end of May, 1940. On May 10th "the balloon went up" and my journal became a day to day – sometimes an hour by hour – account of one of the most dramatic and, from a British point of view, disastrous campaigns of all time – as seen through the eyes of a young soldier. Much of it was written on the move. I was a crew member of a small mobile wireless detachment, and mobile we were! With our division we moved swiftly into Belgium to the pre-determined B.E.F. line just east of Brussels, where we were to hold and repulse the German invaders. Even more speedily we found ourselves, along with the whole B.E.F., forced to retrace bewildered footsteps, until out of the chaos of retreat a defensive line was formed – a sort of deep half circle with a short strip of coast that included the port of Dunkirk providing its northern diameter and boundary. And then, within a few days, the final retreat to Dunkirk, and evacuation from its beaches.

Neither those dramatic final three weeks with the B.E.F. nor the months in France that preceded them can really stand alone and self-contained in their own right. A proper understanding calls for some awareness of the events, the attitudes, the atmosphere of the period; of the context against which young men like myself joined the Territorial Army, and before long found themselves at war; some realisation of how the army prepared us – or failed to prepare us – for active service; of what it was like to be part of the "phoney war", both in England and France.

In telling of these things I am very conscious of the fact that in so doing I am also telling a little of what it was like to be emerging from youth to manhood in the Britain of the late 1930's – a period the like of which has surely never been known before or since.

In providing this background, this context, and in writing of our time in France, which culminated in the evacuation from Dunkirk, my memory has been aided not only by my diary but by contemporary written records – notably the voluminous correspondence between myself and my girl friend (who became my wife in 1946, when I ceased to be a soldier); plus a magnificent scrap book created by my comrade-in-arms the late Harry Sargeant. This fine example of his archivist's feeling for the stuff of which history is made comprises, in the main, extracts from letters which he received and sent during the war years, skilfully welded together and interspersed with many fascinating memorabilia of those times. To his widow Mary, the receiver and sender of most of the letters in question, I offer my warmest thanks for allowing me access not only to a unique source of material, but also to many photographs taken by Harry during the period with which this book is concerned. I am very much indebted to Ken Rider, Clive Tonry, Geoff Newman and Phil Vane, who were kind enough to read through and comment on much of what I have finally included in this book. My wife, who has added to her skills as a librarian those of word-processing, has unfailingly produced order and coherence out of almost unbelievably chaotic manuscript drafts; and Professor Mike Lynch, my old friend and colleague from Sheffield days, has brought about the transformation of her diskettes into the handsome typeface of this small volume. My debt to both of them is great indeed.

Chapter 1

HALL GREEN

It may be that as the years of war were also for some of us the years
when we were very young, we have been apt to confuse the two and
even to feel a sigh of regret when thinking of that time.

Sir Anthony Eden

In 1936 when, as a 16 year old, I joined the staff of the Birmingham
Reference Library, the First World War was not all that far behind us.
My father and uncles had fought in it, and particularly when loosened
up by a drink or two, would tell their favourite stories of life in – and
behind – the trenches: of sergeant majors who really did dock the rum
ration, of the French and their peculiarities, of bombardments and
mines, of boyhood friends who never returned. The Chief Librarian of
the Commercial and Patents Library, to which I was soon transferred,
had been an infantry-man and a sergeant, in the Middle East; he loved
to reminisce, and added his own distinctive and extra dimension to what
I had heard from my father and uncles. By this time, too, following the
immediate post-war decade in which those who had been through
World War I had found it too painful to write about, some quite
outstanding novelists had produced what in many cases turned out to be
enduring works about their war as they had seen it. These I had eagerly
absorbed, along with much of the War Poetry, of which the Birmingham
Reference Library had a quite outstanding special collection.

But before long, like most of my friends and contemporaries, I
began to develop an uneasy awareness that this vicarious interest in war
was more than likely to be sharpened by personal involvement in the

real thing. I would say that from 1937 onwards I had little doubt that war was inevitable, and though I welcomed Munich with the best of them, deep down I could not really believe that anything would come of it, much as I would have liked to do so, and I very soon resumed the hypnotic "Hitler watching" – and listening – that for most of us was an ever present feature of life in those last few pre-war years.

Over the lives of all of us at that time, then, and particularly perhaps those of military age, there was this omnipresent shadow of impending war; but it certainly did not stop us enjoying life to the full. I thoroughly enjoyed my work as a librarian, and in my spare time studied hard and successfully for the examinations leading to a full professional qualification; I was fortunate indeed in my immediate colleagues – for the most part, like-minded youths and girls, many of them of my own age, and sharing similar literary interests; there were staff dances and, on some Sundays, staff rambles; I belonged to a tennis club; I had kept contact with a number of school friends; I had Devonshire walking holidays and holiday camp holidays with my close friend Geoff Newman; life in fact was full, and life was good. But we knew it couldn't last, and this, I suppose, gave something of a tang and urgency to it all.

As 1938 unfolded, the talk, as we ate our lunch-time sandwiches in the male staff common room, was more and more about the possibility of war and of how it might affect us; and this was also becoming the main topic of conversation between Geoff Newman and myself, on our various outings together.

There was much talk in the press of conscription, and in 1939 this was in fact introduced for 20 year olds, by Hore Belisha. Though we were still too young to be affected, this was undoubtedly an additional influence towards a line of thought which Geoff and I – and indeed many of our friends and colleagues – had been developing, as the momentum towards war built up. If war and our involvement in it were inevitable, we argued, then the sensible thing to do was to join the Territorial Army in a unit of our own choice; not – emphatically not – the infantry, the life of whom in the last war was all too clearly known to us; but some other, more congenial branch of the service. By this time there were pressures from many other directions to join the T.A. There was a big recruiting drive by government, and public service employers such as our own were encouraged to release staff on full pay for a fortnight in camp each year. This represented a doubling of our normal two weeks holiday: for holiday is certainly how we envisaged our August camp by the sea-side. Moreover there was a 'joining' bounty of £5 – itself a not inconsiderable inducement, since it represented between 3 and 4 weeks salary for a youngster of my age. More intangible, but very potent indeed, was the feeling that to join the T.A. would be to terminate the agonising indecision about what, if anything, one should be doing: as a territorial soldier the decision would have been made, and one's role in any war that broke out, predetermined.

The ultimate decision in fact more or less made itself, as did the choice of the arm of service. The nearest T.A. unit happened to be in Hall Green, on the main Birmingham-Stratford road, just round the corner from where my friend Geoff Newman lived; it was the 48th Divisional Signals. A near neighbour of the Newmans' was the Adjutant of that unit (a regular officer). Geoff's father had himself been a signaller in the First World War, and saw the Signals as an arm of the service in which he would much sooner see his son serve than the 'P.B.I.'; what's more he knew the Adjutant. Mr. Newman strongly encouraged both of us to join the 48th Divisional Signals, and went so far as to give us Morse code instruction during my weekly Sunday visits to his home. After much heart-searching, and with the support of my own father, who agreed with Mr. Newman's line of reasoning, I enlisted as a Signalman in the 48th Div. Sigs., in February 1939, together of course with Geoff. On such relatively fortuitous considerations were decisions made which determined the next 7 years of our lives – and on which, indeed, might well have hinged the matter of whether or not we survived the war at all!

We were not alone in joining the 48th Divisional Signals; during 1938 and 1939 recruits poured in, and before long the unit was full and a second line unit was created – the 61st Div. Sigs. Amongst my fellow

recruits to the 48th were many school-mates from King Edward's
Grammar School, Camp Hill, including several from my own year, and
in addition there was quite a significant contingent from the various
departments of our Birmingham local authority – not least from the
Public library service to which I myself belonged. In the section of the
Unit to which I was assigned – "A" (Ack) Section – there were five of us
who had been together at school and who at that time – early 1939 –
were all approaching nineteen years of age; in addition there were four
of us who worked in the Reference Library (the Commercial and
Patents branch of it, in my case). Our unit in fact had a great deal in
common with the "Pals" battalions of the First World War.

The business of the 48th Div. Sigs. was to provide the communications
for the 48th Infantry Division, which meant wireless, land lines and
despatch riders, with all appropriate organisational support such as the
signal office and the technical expertise required to maintain electrical
equipment and motor transport. Each of us was expected to master and
qualify in a "trade" and each trade was graded into 3 levels. The highest
regarded and best paid trades were Electrician Signals, and Instrument
Mechanic, graded from A1 (the highest, and well nigh unattainable) to
A3; next came Operator, Wireless and Line – from B1 to B3; and then
lineman (those responsible for laying and maintaining the telegraph/
telephone lines) whose trade was graded as C. The despatch riders – most
of them motor cycle fanatics, all of them highly skilled riders, and some of
them members of the Royal Signals Display Team – were a law unto
themselves, and they commanded a D grading.

My own Section – "A" Section – had two principal tasks: first of all,
providing wireless communication between Divisional Headquarters and
the 3 Infantry Brigade headquarters, via 4 mobile No. 9 radio sets,
housed in wooden horse-box like vehicles which we called "Gin Palaces".
These sets were capable of operating not only when brigades and division
were in fixed locations, but when their vehicles were actually on the
move. The section's second responsibility was to provide a similar service
between Divisional Headquarters and the division's artillery formations.
This called for smaller wireless sets – No. 11 sets, and smaller vehicles –

high powered Humber vans with canvas hoods, known to us as "bugs". The larger gin-palaces had a crew of 3 wireless operators and an electrician signals, one of whom would also act as driver. The smaller bugs had crews of two operator/drivers, who between them had to operate the wireless set and drive the truck for 24 hours a day, charge the set's batteries, cook, and maintain the whole detachment. In the words of Clive Tonry: "Exhaustion guaranteed". I should add that what I have been describing was the establishment according to the book. The reality was that all our training before the outbreak of war, as indeed for some time after, was carried out with scratch equipment and vehicles, much of it old and out-of-date. In this our experience was no different from that of any other section in our unit or, no doubt, from that of any other unit of any other Territorial division.

As members of the Territorial Army we were expected to turn up for training at the Unit's Headquarters at Cateswell House, Hall Green, one evening a week. In addition attendance at a number of weekend exercises was required; and, of course, two weeks at camp, in August. Training included drill – and in this we were not at such a disadvantage as we might have been, because we joined at a time when drilling in formations of four was giving way to formations of three, and we rookies were not much more at sea than the old sweats. Technical training focused mainly on mastering the Morse code, and learning how to tune in, receive and transmit on a radio set, together with all the associated operating procedures.

The key figures in our T.A. unit were the small cadre of regular soldiers – the adjutant, the R.S.M. and a few Permanent Staff Instructors (P.S.I.'s). The officers, from the Commanding Officer downwards, were civilians like ourselves, one or two of the more senior having served in the First World War. They were drawn from a rather more affluent stratum of society than most of the men they commanded – at least, this was my own impression at the time – and some of them gave the T.A. a good deal of their spare time. I do not remember that many of them exhibited any particular military or technical expertise, but with very few exceptions they were pleasant and dedicated men who took their duties seriously and did all that could reasonably be expected of them, and more, when ultimately confronted with the realities of war.

The unit, as I have said, was brought up to full establishment by a great influx of recruits in 1938/39, and numerically these considerably outweighed the hard core of existing Territorial N.C.O.s and other ranks, many of whom had several years of service behind them by the time that we joined. A few of these had relevant specialist civilian expertise – in the Post Office, for example; or in one case, as a ship's radio operator; but on the whole they were drawn from a variety of skilled and unskilled occupations and what they knew of signals and communications had been learned as spare-time soldiers in the T.A. All in all it was a very mixed group that had to be welded together, and before long, as will be seen, it was to become even more so.

Weekend exercises carried out in the Warwickshire and Worcestershire countryside, during the months after we joined up, had left little impression so far as "training for war" was concerned; but they certainly introduced us to some of the more agreeable aspects of life in the services: roaring out army versions of popular songs and ballads from the backs of lorries, as we rattled through the dusty countryside (to this day it is these versions rather than the true and original words that spring immediately to mind if I hear the tunes in question); drinks at rural pubs, all in our uniformed anonymity; and above all, perhaps, getting to know and appreciate our fellow territorials, men whose outlook and background were often very different from ours – men whose paths, in the normal course of civilian existence, would never have crossed our own.

Probably as a consequence of a certain, if limited proficiency in Morse (very much a matter of "In the land of the blind the one eyed man is king") Geoff Newman and I were quite quickly appointed acting, unpaid local lance-corporals – a promotion which even at this distance in time still strikes me as downright extraordinary. I suppose this involved us in certain responsibilities, but the only ones that spring to mind nearly fifty years on are the rousing at 0630 reveille, of the 8 fellow occupants of a bell tent, during our two August weeks in camp at Sheringham; and – an even more onerous responsibility – sharing out, under the eagle and hungry eyes of the soldiers concerned, the contents of a great dixie full of food, with meat in one compartment, potatoes in another, and cabbage in a third. For a 19 year old trainee librarian all of this was indubitably very broadening, as were such things as the rapidly acquired art of taking care of and guarding one's bed-space, kit and possessions. As I recorded in a letter to my girl friend "I've had a knife and my cap pinched, so of course the only thing I could do was pinch someone else's. They'd pinch the milk out of a blind man's tea." In the same letter I recorded that for my first week's labours I had just received the princely sum of 12/6 (62p in present day money). In her reply she professed incredulity that not only was I having this free holiday by the sea, but was even being paid for it!

Holiday in truth it was. It no doubt rained from time to time, but my memories are of golden and care-free days in the open air, in the company of friends old and new, with the portable gramophone of Despatch Rider Corporal Stafford (who had brought to camp his own superb B.M.W. motor-bike) blaring out "And the Angels Sing" and "South of the Border". Some training, at least, we must have carried out, for my letters of that time refer to rising at 0400 to take part in an exercise, Anglia v Saxonia, with shifts on wireless sets – two hours on, two hours off – over a 36 hour period; but it has certainly left no lasting impression. By this time – August 1939 – war was of course only a week or two away, and even the dimmest of us must have realised that before long all this "exercising" would be for real. If we needed confirmation it would have come for some of us around that same time, when the annual Librarians' Summer School, at Birmingham, saw its normally rather sophisticated membership concluding the concert on the last night – albeit somewhat self-consciously – with "There'll always be an England!"

The atmosphere during the latter part of that August was electric with uncertainty and it was in a very real sense a relief to most of us when we knew the die was cast – with Hitler's invasion of Poland on Friday 1 September. So far as people like myself were concerned, this meant we were at war – our country had said crystal clear that we would take up arms if Poland's frontier were violated, and now this had happened. Not until years later did I come to realise that even at that stage there were those amongst our then leaders who were still hoping that in some way they might avoid the final step of declaring war. To us the deferment until Sunday 3rd Sept of the official declaration of war was no more than a rather strangely delayed formality.

On September 1st 1939, then, we put civilian life behind us and reported for duty at the 48th Divisional Signals headquarters at Hall Green. Our notices of mobilisation said that we should bring "such uniform and equipment as had already been issued", plus a number of domestic essentials such as Towels, hand, 1; 6 different kinds of brush (Brushes, blacking, clothes, hair, polishing, shaving, and tooth); 3 pairs of socks; but only 2 pairs of pants! For lending the army a "complete and serviceable set" of these and the other personal possessions on the list, we would in due course each be paid 10/- – provided we were "retained for service". We were also asked to bring enough food to last a day, but this, apparently, was to be at our own expense!

One of my fellow librarians, Harry Sargeant, recorded at the time that on Sept 1st everything at our headquarters was in a state of chaos and disorder. I would concur with that, but my principal recollection is of queuing – queuing into the small hours, in order to complete endless documentation and to be issued with several miscellaneous bits and pieces of all kinds. The excitement and drama of it all sustained us as hour succeeded hour, but long before we were dismissed to our "billet" we were dead weary and ready to drop. Drop we did – on the wooden floor of a church hall a couple of hundred yards away, and with our gas masks immediately at hand, for like everyone else, we confidently expected that Blitzkrieg and aerial bombardment would start from Day 1, with no holds barred. As I lay on those bare boards I thought longingly of my comfortable civilian bed – only a quarter of a mile or so down the hill – but the army's machine was already taking grip of us, and it never seriously occurred to me to chance my luck and take off for home for what was left of that night.

In the days that followed, whenever I could get off duty I would rush off home to sleep, bath and sit in an armchair. Though we were all prepared to put up with anything that the army might provide, in the way of poor food or hard lying – thinking in our ignorance that such wretched conditions were the inevitable lot of the soldier – none of us could easily get into the way of sleeping on floor boards and extracting rest and benefit from it. Desperate tiredness in fact characterised the whole of this early period in Birmingham.

These early days of mobilisation must have been a nightmare for our officers, plucked from the routine of their civilian jobs to take charge of five or six hundred rather bewildered and under-trained men, and they must have been thankful indeed for the breadth of the shoulders of their full-time professional colleagues: the adjutant, the R.S.M. and the P.S.I.'s. Some semblance of order and routine did in fact begin to emerge: there was drill, there were route marches; but precious little, if anything, to do with signals or communications.

It is generally accepted that unlike their fathers at the beginning of the First World War, our generation went into World War II without jingoism and, indeed, with a minimum of overt patriotism of any kind. That said it would be very wrong to underestimate the quiet fury that Hitler and his antics had by this time generated in the Britain of the late 1930's, or the strength of the growing resolve to stop him. For myself, I remember no "king and country" flag-waving, but rather a resigned and realistic acceptance that this was a war that must be fought, that of course we would win it, (how irrational could we get! – but what I write is true) and that it would not be over in five minutes. Detached and hard-boiled about it all we may have been, but as in any war, emotions were sharpened, and a tendency to sentimentalise rose nearer the surface. In our church hall billet, and on our route marches, we would sing the songs of the First World War – songs about "long, long trails a-winding," about "not wanting to go to the trenches no more"; songs that somehow I felt we were not really entitled to sing, because they belonged to an army of the past that had truly earned the right to sing them. Not that I refrained from joining in: it was pleasant indeed to march along the Stratford Road in manly style and in columns of three, deferred to by the traffic, and waved to by the girls from the Beacon Insurance Company and other offices that lined our route.

It was pleasant, too, when a troops concert, extemporised at little or no notice, gave an opportunity for the unsuspected talent concealed in our ranks to emerge and show itself off: a little "dance-band" gave out dreamy sentimental tunes; our own "A" Section produced a most reasonable young tenor with a very sentimental repertoire; and there was some enthusiastic community singing. After the concert was over, I remember being moved to pour out a short poem about the emotions it had evoked in so many of us. Mercifully that poem soon disappeared without trace, but I mention it to make my point: a great deal of emotion was generated at the outbreak of this war, and some of it in the most unlikely quarters.

These very early days in Hall Green were notable for a change in many ways more important in its immediate and long term consequences for our unit than anything that happened before or after. There were posted to us a draft of reservists, together with a few experienced regular soldiers. Without these men, with their long years of experience, their efficiency in their trades, their discipline, and the qualities of character that came from years in the army – much of it overseas in India, Palestine or Egypt – it is difficult to imagine how our unit could ever have become operational, even in home service terms; let alone survive the demands of active service that were to be made of it before many months had passed.

Sixteen of these 'old soldiers' were posted to our own "A" section, and they were to play such an important part in our lives during the months that followed that a little more needs to be said about them and their background. In most cases they had joined the regular army for 8 years of full-time service, followed by 4 years on the reserve. The majority of them were in fact already reservists, in their late 20's or early 30's; but there were one or two still serving their time, and these were rather younger. What came as a great surprise to most of us was the general calibre of these men; more or less without exception they were highly intelligent, very proficient in those trades in which we ourselves were the veriest beginners; and in addition of course they were skilled in the normal soldierly attainments such as foot drill and the handling of weapons. I suppose that for many of us at that time, our image of the regular army soldier had been based on some long outdated stereotype of an old-fashioned infantryman, going back to a time when to join the army was often the last resort of those who were the rejects and drop-outs from the society of their time; sometimes, indeed, service in the army had in those days been an alternative offered by magistrates to a man found guilty of a minor offence, who would otherwise be sent to gaol.

Of the reservists who came to our section, many, probably most, had joined the army after coming onto the labour market in the late 1920's or early 1930's. Unemployment was very high, and the chances of getting a job – particularly in black spots such as Wales and the North of England – were very low indeed. To join a technical branch of the army, such as Signals, gave them not only several years of security, but the opportunity to learn a skilled trade which could well lead to employment on rejoining civilian life. In addition, of course, there were all the traditional attractions of the army for a youngster at that time: an open-air life, plenty of sport, and the prospect of service in some of those many exotic countries of the world which at that time were still marked red on the map. By the later 1930's, when many of the reservists had finished their full time engagements with the army, the employment situation, under the spur of re-armament, had picked up markedly, and most of them – often by that time married and with young children – were beginning to create a very satisfactory niche for themselves in civilian life. Amongst those who joined us, for example, was one who was making great strides as a Post Office engineer; another who was a wireless operator on flying boats, with the prestigious Imperial Airways; at least one was a foreman; there was a wireless operator who before being recalled to army life had worked from the world-famous Rugby transmitter; and many more of similar character. For all of these reservists, to be called back into the army in their late 20's, or 30's, to have to abandon the new life they were laboriously building up for themselves, must have been a shock more rude and sickening than anything experienced by most of their Territorial Army comrades in arms. They were, of course, once-bitten men, who knew all about the army; they had no illusions about what this war business was about; and they expressed their views not only with force but with a cynical, at times spectacularly profane, humour that filled most of us young Territorials with spell-bound admiration. Their influence on all of us was tremendous – and enduring; and to this day I retain a vivid recollection of each and every one of them.

Probably because it represented our very first days as full-time soldiers, that immediately post-mobilisation period in Birmingham, when the reservists first joined us, still looms larger than is warranted by its duration. In fact in no time at all, the many rumours that had spread were confirmed, and we left Birmingham for an "unknown destination". This, we thought was war indeed, and we were not backward in exercising our quickly acquired soldiers' prerogative of grumbling – why the hell, we asked, was it necessary to go miles from home to do our training: what was wrong with Hall Green and Cateswell House? But really we were well enough aware that soldiering within a short walk or a tram-ride of home was not a very sensible or satisfactory state of affairs. On 14th September, then, a fleet of coaches arrived to bear us into the "unknown", and we left Birmingham behind us.

Chapter 2

CHILTON FOLIAT

The departure from Birmingham began in a way which we soon came to realise was inseparable from any move with the army: a reveille at an unbelievable small hour of the morning. At 0345 we were roused for a trip which turned out to be some 90 miles. It was more than 10 hours later, at 1400 hours, when we finally arrived!

We proceeded south, through glorious Cotswold hills that were looking at their early autumn best. The sun was shining, and for me a truly ironic twist to the situation was that instead of driving through this countryside in a not too comfortable coach full of soldiers, I should at just about that time in September have been happily hiking through it – leading the Public Libraries' annual long-distance ramble. In preparation for this, Geoff Newman (who for this sort of purpose had long been accepted as an honorary librarian), and I, had in fact devoted the previous Easter to carrying out a 4 days recce. of the proposed route.

In 1939 we were, of course, very much countryside-starved town boys and some of us at least were quite well pleased when our coach pulled up at a final destination set in rural surroundings fully equal to the Cotswold country that we had been driving through. We had halted at a lodge which guarded the entrance to a magnificent estate on the perimeter of a small and picturesque village on the Berkshire/Wiltshire border – Chilton Foliat. Just round the corner from this lodge was a tiny hamlet of estate-worker's cottages, and beyond these was a delightful rural walk which led to the metropolis of Hungerford, a couple of miles or so away.

Our officers disappeared up the long drive which led to Chilton Manor itself; the troops dismounted from their coach, strolled around, smoked, appraised what they saw, and discussed the possible options for our billets. When the officers returned, with the decision made, the outcome was to say the least something of a surprise. Just inside the estate, on the opposite side of the road to the lodge and the various outbuildings associated with it, was a fairly large barn-like structure with a thickly thatched roof. It was constructed of stout wood, except that at the front the barn was completely open save for two or three uprights which supported the roof, and across which was stretched wire netting. It was clear from the state of the earth floor that its occupants until quite recently had been chickens! It was also being used to store quite a collection of miscellaneous junk. This, we were told, was our billet. With little pretence to originality we christened it the 'fowl pen': it was to be our home for the next four months!

I have already said that we Territorials had little or no idea of what sort of conditions we could expect now that we were full-time soldiers, and on the whole we took this latest development in our stride. The reservists of course knew differently, and their complaining ("ticking" in the vernacular of that time) knew no bounds. They ticked about our accommodation from morn till night, and to whoever would listen. But in fact, after the initial shock, it was not too bad.

Except where the roof sloped down to near ground level at the back, the fowl pen was quite a reasonably lofty building, and the thick thatch was leak-proof. True it was draughty, but even that was remedied to some extent when after 10 days or so the open front was boarded up; though of course we lost light in the process. As for the bare earth floor, after a thorough cleaning out of the whole building, it seemed much more acceptable, and in true soldierly fashion most of us had in no time at all scrounged old doors, boards, and the like – mostly from a junk heap behind our fowl-pen – and these, when supported by a brick at each corner, raised our sleeping bodies a few inches from the ground.

There was, however, one major drawback to this billet: the thatch was infested with rats. We loathed these creatures, the only matter in doubt being whether we loathed them most of all when they woke us up by running across our blanket-covered bodies as we lay on our boards, or when we could hear the magnified sound of them scuttling underneath us, in the brick-high gap between our bed boards and the earthen floor. A lesser drawback to the fowl-pen was that with more than 20 men accommodated in it, our bed boards had to be so close together that to move about the billet at all was quite a feat of navigation.

Our location in the fowl-pen meant that whatever else might be lacking, we in "A" section need never be short of exercise, for the cook-house, and the marquees which had been erected as mess tents, were situated near to Chilton Manor itself; and that was nearly half a mile distant, at the end of a main drive which climbed quite steeply most of the way. We trod that route, there and back, thrice daily, and except when it rained we quite enjoyed it: the outward journey because it took us through magnificent parkland with stately trees that during our time at Chilton gradually changed to a full autumnal splendour; the return journey because as we came down from the high ground on which the Manor – and our cook-house – were situated, we could see glorious countryside rolling away in the distance, bounded by a range of enticing low hills full of promise for off-duty rambles. But it must be said that the joys of the return journey were not exclusively aesthetic; the walk back from meals was also the occasion for keenly looked-forward to competition. Using our large, flat army-issue tin plates as 'Frisbees' – we would see who could complete the journey back from the cook-house in the minimum number of skims, with a penny-a-head kitty as prize for the fortunate winner.

It is a tribute to the hunger generated by our open-air life that we bothered to undertake the quite lengthy walk to the cook-house at all, for the food was appalling. Not that there was any shortage of rations. On the contrary: at that time the eggs, butter, meat which before long would be stringently rationed were available to our army cooks in abundance. The problem was that they were even less competent in their trade as cooks than we were in ours, as 'Operators, Wireless and Line', and our meals were a continuing and sorry tale of good food being ruined by bad cooking. It was, I suppose, at this time that I first heard posed that well-known army question "who called the cook a clot?" and the rejoinder "who called the clot a cook?" (Though a considerably less polite word than 'clot' was normally used). It can not have been entirely without significance that before long, even at that very tolerant early stage in hostilities, our unit's sergeant cook, normally to be seen shirt sleeved and as filthy as a sweep, had been shorn of all 3 of his stripes!

From the shortcomings of the army's cooking there sprang an indirect consequence which perhaps did more for morale, more to bind "A" section together as a group in its own right, than any of the more official approaches to morale-building dreamed up by the powers-that-be. Under the leadership of the reservists – practical men, with an eye for the true priorities – we quickly set to and created our own unofficial cook-house in the open space behind our fowl-pen, using for this purpose the junk of all sorts that littered the whole area. Here, every evening, a huge pot would be set boiling in preparation for supper at 8 o'clock. Everyone would sit or stand around to eat, chat, smoke, gripe, and generally socialise. As time passed and the evenings became too cold to eat comfortably in the open air we would take our food to what we called the Funk-hole – a long low brick-lined tunnel, open-ended and semi-circular in section, that penetrated quite deeply into a grassy bank not far behind the fowl pen and on the perimeter of our cook-house area. Magnificent log fires in a huge fire place made the Funk-hole a very cosy dining room indeed. During day-time it served as a 'classroom' for practising Morse-code on collapsible army tables, but it was during the evenings, at supper time, that it really came into its own.

Our cook-house was presided over by a very remarkable character, Dick Ellis, and it was known to us as Dirty Dick's Cafe. Dick was only 21, but had crammed into his short lifetime more varied – and often highly dubious – experience than comes the way of most men three times his age. Small, dark, with a pencil thin moustache, an engaging leer, a mouth-organ always at the ready, and an inexhaustible fund of stories, Dick had spent some years at sea as a ship's wireless operator. He was in fact very competent at this trade, but by his own account he was more often in trouble than out of it, and either by choice or as a punishment seemed to have spent more time in the galley than in the wireless cabin. Not long before the outbreak of war he had left the sea, come home to Birmingham, and joined the T.A. He certainly knew how to cook, and the delicious odours from his pot drew us like a magnet as the hour of supper drew nearer. The basics for the meal were purchased from a kitty to which we all contributed, but Dick's nightly concoctions were not restricted to what this money could buy. All sorts of things went into his cauldron: always a rabbit, or a pheasant, enquiries about the origins of which would elicit a hideous cackle from the ex-sea-cook; sometimes a joint of meat; always a good mixture of vegetables; and sometimes, we swore, a hedgehog. Small wonder that this unofficial meal soon became the gastronomic and social highlight of our day.

Quite rapidly, at Chilton Foliat, the 3 groups which made up our "A" Section – old Territorials, new Territorials, and Reservists – began to shake down into a single community, and something of a corporate identity and spirit began to emerge. Friendships were made, and though the Reservists because of their age and shared experience of the regular army, at first tended to stick together, this broke down as the weeks passed, and on many an evening it was a completely mixed group that adjourned for a night out at favourite pubs in Chilton Foliat or Hungerford. I myself was particularly fortunate in having several friends of long standing within "A" Section. Three of these were colleagues from Birmingham Reference Library, all of whom I knew well, and liked: Ken Rider, Ken Boodson and Harry Sargeant. These three were a few years older than me, but there were 4 others – all 19 year-olds like myself – who had been my contemporaries at the local grammar school. All five of us had lived very near to one another, and four of us had gone on from school to work for the local authority: Clive Tonry in the Electric Supply Department, Phil Vane in the City Surveyors', Maurice Brett in the Parks Department and I myself in the Public Library Service; the fifth, Geoff Newman, was a trainee accountant. Clive and Geoff had been my close friends all through the school years, and after; and though not quite so close to Phil and

Maurice, I had seen quite a bit of them in the years since leaving school. Within "A" Section we 5 became a very close-knit group indeed, spending much of our off duty time together, occupying adjacent bed boards in the 'Fowl pen', and very frequently forming a convenient target for fatigues. We were young, pretty irresponsible, full of high spirits, and quite unable to take this soldiering business too terribly seriously. As I can clearly see, with hindsight, we must have been something of a thorn in the flesh of those in authority.

Our section officer, Lieutenant Lee, was a keen, rugger-playing, outdoor type; he had his personal rifle and was in many respects one's idea of a good infantry officer. He was not particularly strong on the specialist, wireless, side of things, but he really did care about his men and their welfare – probably more so than any other officer in our unit – and he was understandably popular with all of us. Our section sergeant was a territorial of many years standing, a man of rather colourless personality, and not a particularly strong character. His position vis-à-vis the reservists could obviously not have been very comfortable, and in general, they ran rings round him. He was, however, supported by a lance-sergeant of a very different stamp – Frank Gattrell, a man of about 40 who sported the "rooty gong" – the long service and good conduct medal which rewarded 18 years of regular army service or, as the soldiery would have it "18 years of undetected crime". Frank had left the army shortly before the outbreak of war, and then joined our Territorial unit. He was a likeable, outgoing character, wily as only an old soldier could be, and though his specialisation was not so much signals as motor transport, he was a very considerable asset to the section.

The junior N.C.O.s – corporals and lance-corporals – were most of them Territorials of fairly long standing. They were pleasant men but were naturally light on experience and training at that early stage in the war. Quite understandably the reservists were none too happy about being subordinate to N.C.O.s so manifestly their inferiors in every aspect of signals and soldiering, and did not hesitate to say so. Before long some Territorial N.C.O.s lost their stripes, including –

quite rightly – Geoff and myself, who were in any case only acting, unpaid local lance-corporals, and several of the reservists were promoted. In combination with the one or two of them who already held N.C.O. rank when they joined us, this gave the section a reservist N.C.O. in charge of nearly every wireless detachment, and where a Territorial N.C.O. did remain as detachment commander there was always at least one experienced reservist 'other-rank' to support him. This deployment of our reservists and the promotion of several of them was so obviously the right way to use their skills and experience that it was accepted with good grace by all concerned, and the section was immeasurably the stronger for it. At a fairly early stage there occurred another change of personnel – but this time of a relatively minor character. It had been decided that men under 19 would not be sent overseas, and as overseas was pretty clearly our division's intended destination, "A" section lost its few members who came into this category.

Settling into our new life affected us in different ways. The pangs of parting from homes and families were certainly deeply felt by all, in those early days, but particularly by those with wives and young children. Harry Sargeant described in his first letter from Chilton Foliat to his wife-to-be a church parade which took us to Chilton's beautiful old 13th century church. The highly evocative organ music, the sun streaming in through the ancient stained glass, the atmosphere generated by a church full of uniformed men, newly at war – all of these things built up to something both poignant and thrilling; and Harry records all the troops as being deeply moved, so much so that for the first mile of the march back to billets, not a word was to be heard from anyone. Most of the men found an outlet for their feelings of separation by frequent letter writing – in 1939 telephones at home were not the commonplace that they are today – and all looked forward with the greatest of eagerness to weekend leaves which took us back to Birmingham every two or three weeks. All, that is, except some of the reservists, who rarely if ever put in for weekend passes. The reason for this, as we eventually came to realise, was that for most of them home was considerably further away than Birmingham, and since these weekends did not qualify for free rail warrants, the fare made too deep an inroad into their pay for more than a very occasional weekend off to be contemplated. True, they were more accustomed than the rest of us to separation from their homes and families, but it must have seemed yet another twist of the knife to men who had believed their soldiering days to be behind them.

For all of us, however, there was one great blessing that softened and eased our entry into army life: 1939 produced a most glorious Indian summer. In September and much of October golden day succeeded golden day, and the memories that come back are all of sunshine and open air: eating in the open air; practising Morse in the open air; reading my pocket Shakespeare, and dozing, sprawled out on the grass patch in front of the fowl pen, during our lengthy lunch breaks. And with the fowl pen as our bed-room, it would be not too far removed from the truth to add to this list, sleeping in the open air. What to me seemed quite remarkable at the time, and still does, was the fact that during the whole of this period at Chilton Foliat – which was certainly not all golden Indian summer – I was healthier than I had ever been in my life, with not even so much as a hint of a cough or a sneeze.

As a way of life the daily round in our new existence could scarcely have been more different from that which we had left behind us. A characteristically graphic summary from Harry Sargeant had it that "we are settling down to a routine of Morse, driving, digging, cooking, shooting, drilling, wireless, marching, eating, smoking, sleeping (very little) and swearing and cursing". To this I personally would add gambling, drinking and – with considerable feeling – fatigues! Some of these activities, at least, merit a little elaboration.

The Morse code, of course, was central to all the activities of the wireless section – "Ack" Section – to which we belonged. Learning it was not difficult for anyone with a reasonable memory, and with practice it was possible to achieve quite a decent speed – at least so far as receiving and reading Morse was concerned. Moving through from a speed of four words a minute, onwards and upwards to ten, came pretty easily;

and fifteen words a minute was a not unrealistic expectation for most of us. Transmitting Morse intelligibly was however a different matter: this called for a delicacy of touch that not all of us possessed, and even the transmitting of a few of the reservists left something to be desired. All the same, most of them could both receive and transmit at an adequate twenty words a minute and the best of them were way up in the higher twenties, with in some cases a machine-like precision that was almost indistinguishable from automatic transmission.

At an altogether lower level in the day's round, but quite enjoyable in its way, was digging – digging everything from trenches to latrines, from pits for the burial of rubbish to shallow trenches round the huge marquees that sprang up around the cookhouse and headquarters areas to which we walked for all our meals. It was an eye-opener to most of us to learn that there is a right way and a wrong way to hold a pick or a shovel for maximum efficiency and minimum liability to strain or injury, just as there is a right and wrong way to lift the heavy boxes, pieces of equipment and the like that army life seemed to keep in a state of perpetual motion. There was something very satisfying about a piece of well executed digging, just as there was about a cleanly received or transmitted message in Morse – and both the art of digging and the use of the Morse code have in common with riding a bicycle the fact that although they may grow rusty with lack of practice, once learned they are with one for life, and can fairly quickly be polished.

To us the most glamorous – and certainly, in the long term, the most useful skill that the army required us to acquire was that of driving. In those days car ownership was rare indeed, and very much a status symbol. The matter of learning to drive simply didn't arise for most of us, but once called up for service in a mobile wireless section we very swiftly found ourselves being initiated into the mysteries of gear changing, double declutching, reversing and the like – and (minimally) the workings of the "engine i.c.". Our instructor was the amiable Corporal Joe Greenhalgh – a reservist who prior to his recall had been an A.A. man. His approach was very much that of the deep-end: into the driving seat and away you went, to the accompaniment of a running commentary from our instructor. Joe's nerves must have been made of steel: I recall driving down Hungerford main street – to the peril of all abroad, as usual – and losing my wits and nerve completely as we approached the T junction which was the main London road. I forgot how to stop, how to slow down, how to turn left or right, and was simply driving on a dead straight, undeviating course, which would have plunged me at right angles directly into the busy main road traffic. Joe's patient and ever-ready right arm shot out, applied the huge hand-brake in the nick of time, and all was well. Every one of Joe's 'trainees' could I am sure, record a similar anecdote: no wonder he was always ready for his beer in the evening!

For some strange reason it was decided that once we were considered to have mastered the business of driving, we should each be issued with a 5/- civilian driving licence, and by early November we were deemed ready to receive these. Considering our totally inadequate experience and extremely limited skill this was an extraordinary, not to say hair-raising decision, but within a week or so it was to be put to the test in a manner which only the army could have perpetrated. Suddenly (such happenings always came out of the blue) a group of us were detailed to drive a number of hired cars, which were due for return to Newbury, some 12 miles away. The immediate removal by the troops of any desirable and detachable unconsidered trifles such as mirrors or clocks took place in a routine manner which by this time was no surprise to any of us, though the unsuccessful attempt by one of our number to remove his car's steering wheel for his small son to play with actually did raise an eyebrow or two. The transfer of the cars to Newbury was relatively uneventful, but it then transpired that stage two would be to collect from the race course some of our unit's long awaited complement of motor transport. An N.C.O. pointed to one of these – a huge six-wheeled army vehicle – and told me it was mine, for delivery to Chilton. Just getting it started was difficult enough; driving it through Newbury was a nightmare, and perhaps it was as well that neither then nor for the rest of the journey back did I succeed in getting it into a higher gear than second. Compared with the wireless trucks – "gin-palaces" – on which our limited driving experience had been gained, these giants seemed like battleships. That I missed a turning (no question of being in convoy – it was every man for himself) and went for two miles in the wrong direction did not exactly speed my progress and neither did at least eight stops, mostly to allow the engine to cool down from the heat generated by its second gear progress. It was therefore something of a relief to me to find that in spite of all, there were many who had started before me and had yet to arrive, having broken down on the way. The truck which I myself had driven was in fact brand new, but most of the rest were said to be of vintage c.1926. From this motley array, one odd man out was a fine private car – requisitioned, or perhaps purchased, for senior officer use. It was, as I recollect it, a Lanchester, and the lucky driver was Geoff Newman who promptly succeeded in locking the free wheel on the overdrive. Exactly what this meant we were not sure, except that it was clearly a bad thing to have done! Like all the rest of our unit's transport these Newbury vehicles – or what was left of them – were to be inherited by the Germans some six months or so later, so perhaps it was something of a blessing that we had already begun to ensure that the state in which the enemy would find them was very far from pristine.

Driving and learning the Morse code, plus a certain amount of wireless and operational procedures were, then, the main focus of our "technical" training activities in those early weeks of the war, but in Harry Sargeant's list he rightly included shooting as an item in the routine we had settled into. There was, however, precious little of this, and the memories that remain are not so much of improving proficiency and higher scores as of miserable hours on the range, waiting for one's turn to shoot; and even more miserable hours afterwards boiling out our rifles and wistfully thinking of the metal gauze – forbidden, it was said, on pain of 'jankers', or worse – that would have made the whole process of cleaning the rifle barrel after firing so very much easier!

An item in Harry Sargeant's list that did feature pretty prominently in the training schedule was route marches – often, it seemed to us, because the powers that be had run out of ideas on what to do with us.

More often than not these route marches were not what they might have seemed, especially if led by the wily old soldier who was our section's lance-sergeant. He would lead us off from the fowl pen very smartly, and at a good pace, along a Chilton country lane; but a couple of bends and a quarter of a mile or so later he would fall us out in a secluded copse just adjacent to the lane, and the section would smoke, gossip and gamble away the time that the 'route march' was expected to take. 'Younger' soldiers were not slow to catch on, and lance-corporal Harry Sargeant records the night exercise when he and his detachment of 3 were dropped off at a particular point and ordered to get back to billets on foot, via Old Hayward – a total journey of 4 miles. In fact he brought his men back the direct way – a comfortable 25 minutes walk ; and even then he found that most of the other groups had got back in front of him.

That Harry's list of the activities which filled our day made no reference to fatigues is perhaps accounted for by the fact that as a junior N.C.O. he was not so near the sharp end of these as those of us who made up the rank and file. Certainly for our little clique of 5 who had been at school together fatigues loomed very large indeed, and not least the cook-house with its time honoured "spud-bashing". Often, however, there were compensations in the form of extra food – a loaf, some bacon, a pound of butter (meant for the officers), scrounged from the cooks as legitimate "perks". Cook-house apart, there were always stores to be moved, the open-air ablutions to be scrubbed out, latrines to be emptied, vehicles to be cleaned, marquees to be put up or taken down. The latter exercise seemed always to take place on Sunday, the so-called day of rest, and together with church parade this would usually account for a whole morning, often stretching into the afternoon – one Sunday, indeed, on returning from Church we were detailed to put up 8 marquees which had blown down during Saturday night – a job that dragged on till 5p.m.! The prescribed drill for erecting and taking down a marquee was complex and called for a fair number of pairs of hands. We suspected, with some justification, that the 5 of us got more than our share of this particular fatigue, and since an important

Front cover of original Diary bought in France and Marked Agenda 1940.

Original Diary 28th May. At Chateau in Wormhout. Note French page headings.

Original Diary writing. On the Beach at Dunkirk 29th/30th May.
Note that the Diary entry overruns the allotted space for May.

Service book for the author (AB64).

Service book for the author (AB64).

Signalman Wilf Saunders 1939.

Harry Sargeant, Wilf Saunders & Ken Rider at T.A. Camp August 1939.

Drill Practice.

Clive Tonry at Sheringham T.A. Camp August 1939.

Geoff Newman & Wilf Saunders pictured at Territorial Army Camp –
Sheringham in August 1939.

gastronomic event each week was a magnificent Sunday lunch down in Hungerford at The Lamb (purchased at a cost of 2/- – a not inconsiderable proportion of the 8/6 which most of us drew as our week's pay) we would go to some lengths to avoid being seen by the section sergeant and caught for Sunday fatigues. More often than not we were unsuccessful, but in such cases we were perfectly capable of disappearing the moment the sergeant's back was turned. Indeed our little group considered work-dodging, or "scrounging", to be great fun, and something to be expected of a soldier: undoubtedly one of the reasons for our being a prominent target when the sergeant was looking for bodies to do a particular job. But on some occasions at least the fatigues were spread more evenly. Such an occasion was Armistice Day 1939, when I recorded with disgust that our whole unit was paraded in full marching order – packs, tin hats, rifles – and after standing in the cold for a full hour while the officers conferred (and missing the two minutes silence in the process) the outcome of their deliberations was at last revealed: the whole unit was split up, assembled into lines, and … was detailed to pick up paper!

For our group of 5 nineteen year olds this was all a far cry from the Birmingham Council House Department or the Public Libraries and there is no doubt that the sheer novelty of it all helped carry us through those early months. Plus, of course, the irrepressible exuberance of youth – personified above all, perhaps, in Clive who, as I put it at the time, "excelled in noise". His abundant and restless energy would prompt him from time to time to leap in the air for no apparent reason, clap his feet, and bellow "whiroo" – the signal for the rest of us to fall upon him and pin him down: no easy matter, for he was a hefty and muscular youth. For my own part I recall stirring him from slumber one night to inform him that I was still awake, which moved him to swear he would wake me up later, when he was due to go on guard. At about 0030 he did so, and told me I was to report for cook-house duties at 0730. Naturally I ignored this – but it happened to be true, and I suffered accordingly.

Guard duty itself was, in those early days, a pretty light-hearted affair, but never more so than on the occasion of the "wetting" of Alan

Goodanew's second stripe. We territorials had just received our long overdue bounty – a princely £5 – and it seemed proper to us to mark the elevation from lance corporal to corporal of Alan, a reservist, by taking him to the local hostelry and plying him with the strongest brew available – 5 X's at 1/8 a pint. A whisky added to his beer finished off this process very nicely and we were just moving towards a second wind when someone remembered that Alan was in charge of the guard that night, and I was first man on duty. By then it was a good half hour after the time when guard should have been mounted and we were some two miles from our base. We rolled back in a very happy state and the new corporal – mindful no doubt of his regular army days (for this was certainly not the practice at Chilton Foliat) – ceremonially mounted us. As first on duty I composed myself in our home-made sentry box at the entrance to the Chilton Estate and went straight off to sleep. The next thing I was aware of was a colossal, confused roar, and my sentry box began to move wildly from side to side: the balance of the revellers had returned and were hell bent on overturning the box. Apart from a lot of leg-pulling this transgression attracted no consequences, but I shudder to think what would have happened to me if caught in such a situation when the war was a few months older!

After doing a guard duty it was normal to be excused from all duties the next day. The countryside was still a delight to many of us, and on these "excused duty" occasions Geoff Newman and I would often up and away, our packs on our backs, for a good long hike into the nearby hills. We loved the rich variety of shades in the early morning sky, the fascinating lumps of mist in the hollows, the autumnal tints of the magnificent trees and the black sweeps of earth which replaced the corn stacks as new ploughing got under way.

Less idyllic, of course, was life in our fowl pen as colder winds began to blow and November rain made the long walk to get our meals a muddy purgatory. However, some improvements in our conditions did eventually take place. To our total incredulity it emerged that at least one of the many rumours which constantly circulated around our section was true; early in November we were issued with beds – crude and wooden framed, it was true, but an immense advance on the doors supported by bricks that had served us up to that time; and even more unbelievable – each of us was allocated a "mattress" – in the form of a palliasse, and straw to fill it with! However, there was no way in which the army could remedy one of the major problems that most of us encountered: the sheer impossibility of writing letters home against the din and uproar created by a couple of dozen men talking, singing, gambling and generally relaxing in the fowl pen, a difficulty compounded by the fact that there was not so much as a square inch of table or similar flat writing surface! The solution, for most of us, was to repair to the local church hall, which had been turned into a very decent canteen and recreation room – by no means as noisy as the fowl pen, and adequately supplied with writing tables.

At an altogether higher level a break from the fowl pen could be achieved by walking into Hungerford to the Bear Hotel. Here one found a marvellous old lounge with a big fireplace and a roaring log fire, comfortable settees, a parrot who said a refained "hullo" and a waiter, immaculate in tails, and willing to look indulgently on the soldiery who made two half pints last an entire evening. But this was not all the "Bear" had to offer. Once a week we would spend a shilling on a hot bath in one of its sumptuous bathrooms and wallow luxuriously in unlimited hot water; a huge bath towel was provided, to finish off the process. Sadly, inevitably, this could not go on for ever; the time came when the "Bear" was made "Officers only", and put out of bounds to the troops.

The weeks ticked by; we were settling into our new routines; and we were swiftly – and cynically – coming to terms with the army and its ways. In the words of one of our reservists "If your mother was dying of convulsions you would get no sympathy in the army: they would laugh like hell". A more general summing up of the situation, familiar to most ex-servicemen, was that once you were in the army they could and would do anything to you except put you in the family way. It was certainly my own view at the time that within a matter of weeks I had changed immeasurably: my speech had coarsened; my outlook was incredibly wider; worldly knowledge had reached, as I then saw it, the ultimate peak; and, above all, I was beginning to acquire a very much overdue independence and ability to look after myself – two characteristics which developed slowly in a 'mother and sister pampered' youth.

In the wider world, what later came to be known as the "phoney war" was getting under way. Petrol was rationed (and was 1s. 6d a gallon), the sinking of the Royal Oak in mid-October created a stir, as did the reported shooting down of 4 German planes in Scotland; spirits soared with the sinking of the Graf Spee; by late October rationing was imminent, though the French were already on two meatless days a week; cinemas had re-opened in September, but no-one was allowed in without a gas-mask; the newspapers reported that the Germans were dropping spies by parachute into the British lines; and nearer our door-step the local Army Service Corps was reputed to have captured one.

"Phoney" as this first phase may have been, it certainly concentrated the minds of those in our section who were contemplating matrimony, and scarcely a week went by without the banns for one or more of our fellow soldiers being read at the Church parade in Chilton Foliat. The background to each of these early war-time marriages was undoubtedly unique and special to those concerned, but two of them were so very different that they have made quite a lasting impression on this writer. The fascination of the first was probably due to the fact that we had "lived with it" in the fowl pen from the time, some seven weeks before, when the potential groom had first met the lady in question. Night after night, before finally going off to sleep he would debate with all those comrades within earshot whether he should keep his motor-bike, which he treasured, or sell it and get spliced. In the end love triumphed. The banns were duly read, and yet another military wedding took place in Chilton Foliat's beautiful old church. The second memorable marriage was that of one of my librarian colleagues – Harry Sargeant. At the time of the call-up he was approaching 25, and was engaged to a fellow librarian. He had decided from the beginning that the life of a soldier in war-time must be particularly hellish for anyone who was married – it was bad enough, he wrote to his fiancée, for anyone who was only engaged! Not many weeks later this line of thought was reversed in a spectacular (and I am bound to say, quite uncharacteristic) fashion. Harry acted as best man to fellow librarian Ken Boodson, who was the same age as himself, and also engaged to a colleague in the public library service. This moved Harry to throw all caution to the winds. He sent a telegram to his fiancée proposing immediate marriage, was accepted, and on December 20th 1939 was married by special licence, back in Birmingham.

By that time we had been at war for nearly four months and there had been a number of very significant developments in the affairs of our unit, some of which undoubtedly influenced decisions such as those which had led our fellow soldiers into the married state rather earlier than they had intended. The evolution of most of these developments could be traced via one of the most deep-rooted characteristics of the regular soldier – one which soon re-awoke in our section's reservists, and quickly spread to the rest of us. This was the habit of idle but avid speculation on matters which affected our tight little military community: rumours as to promotions, postings and the like; but above all, speculation as to the ultimate destination of the 48th Div. Sigs., and possible embarkation dates. Always there would be someone who claimed to have "all the inside 'griff' my lads". France was certainly the hot favourite, though some of the reservists with whom nostalgia probably carried more weight than reason, would produce elaborate theories as to why Egypt, Malta or even Gibraltar was a more likely destination. The hottest news before the emergence of the final "real griff" was leaked down to us from one of our gunner regiments which had allegedly been shooting so brilliantly that the 48th Division's move to France could only be a matter of days.

Eventually, about the end of November it became apparent even to the most inexperienced eye that "something was up". We had already had our T.A.B. and T.T. inoculations; we began to apply camouflage paint to our vehicles; stores flowed in; red tabs appeared around the place; our tiny tin-pot exercises increased in number; and we were subjected to trial marches in full battle order. But final confirmation that movement was imminent came in the pleasantest of all possible ways: it was announced that not only were we to receive ten full days of glorious leave, but that they were to include the Christmas period. What rejoicings! What plans, what writings of letters to wives and girl friends! Of all my leaves during the seven years I spent in the army, this was without doubt the most eagerly looked forward to, and I would guess that this was equally true of most of my fellow inhabitants of the Fowl Pen.

But before the big day itself there were other pointers to the shape of things to come. Our honorary colonel – "a general somebody or other", as I was later to record it, "gave us the good old platitudes", one day. Much more to the point, and very much appreciated, was an address to the whole unit by our own Commanding Officer, in Hungerford's Corn Exchange. He told us that this would probably be the last time during the war when the whole of 48th Div. Sigs. would be assembled together as one unit. (He was wrong, but how could he possibly have forecast the events which led to a later such gathering, in June 1940). He warned us about the perils of "split-arsed" driving on the French pavé, and the "wrong" side of the road. He told us we would soon be issued with live ammunition, but would probably not be in action for some time, since the Spring of 1940 was expected to produce zero hour. For those of us in "Ack" Section one particularly interesting piece of information was that wireless had not yet been used in France except for training purposes, the reason for this being that lines were considered safer, since enemy direction finding (D/F) apparatus was capable of locating a transmitter immediately. In mobile warfare, of course, when a division was constantly on the move (whether forwards or backwards), wireless simply had to be used, so this was one bit of news from the C.O. that was not exactly received with rapturous enthusiasm.

Our Commanding Officer, a middle-aged to elderly veteran of World War I, was well liked and respected by the troops, as indeed were most of his fellow officers, but it has to be said that our first few months of war-time service had made most of us very conscious of the great gulf between officers and other ranks, and the difference in conditions and treatment rankled not a little. Nothing brought this out more clearly perhaps, than an Officer's Mess menu card, written in a fine italic hand, acquired and preserved by Harry Sargeant. It read as follows:

48 Div Sigs.
Dinner
14/12/39

Brown Windsor

Grilled Fillet of Plaice

Roast Pheasant

Bread Sauce

Baked Potatoes and Brussel Sprouts

Christmas Pudding

Sardine Parmesan

Dessert

Coffee

On the back of this menu Harry had written:

Men's Mess

14/12/1939

Bread

Butter

Meat Paste

It would, however, be wrong to make too much of the irritation which such stark contrasts produced amongst us at that time, for the imminence of our embarkation leave had pushed most other thoughts from our minds. Great plans had been made, and when the day of all days arrived we could forgive the army almost anything – even the fact that in accordance with what by then we had come to realise was a hallowed military tradition, we were woken at an unbelievably early hour and, after much swearing and exhortation by our wretched section sergeant, were formed up for the long march to Hungerford station, laden with every single item of our kit, and looking like colossal Christmas trees. The Birmingham train, which of course was the target for 90% of our unit, was invaded by a horde of excited soldiery, clumsy in all their equipment, but tolerantly beamed upon by the odd one or two civilians in the unreserved part of the train, to whom soldiers were still something of a novelty. We were off! The five of us, naturally in the same compartment, were as bubbling as kids at a Sunday School treat!

I shall never forget that leave. It got off immediately on the right foot. I arrived home. There was a fire. By the fire was an armchair; and the wireless was playing the soft sweet kind of music to which in those days I was much addicted. Off came about two hundredweight of kit: I sank back into the unbelievable luxury of a real armchair – and relaxed.

Our plans for the ten days included one entirely "stag" evening, when the five of us would meet in town, consume several large pints, and follow up with a slap-up dinner and a show. After that, a few more drinks and so to bed. In the event, that was exactly how it did work out! Another evening at the theatre was to be spent with my family and girl friend Joan – the first time they had met her; I had also earmarked one full day to be spent on a ramble with her in our local Warwickshire countryside – to make up, as I put it, for the ramble I should have been leading just after war broke out.

Christmas Day was spent quietly at home, the quietness being particularly marked around lunch-time when there was a broadcast which included "our troops in the Maginot Line". Boxing Day was a different matter altogether. In accordance with what had become a family tradition the evening saw all the younger members off to a dance. This year, for the first time, the group was enlarged to include Joan, my younger sister's boy friend Ted Lane (also a 48 Div. Sigs. 19-year old, though not in "A" Section), and Geoff Newman with his girl friend. With my elder sister and her husband we made up quite a party, and spent a glorious evening tearing round the dance floor to the strains of Donkey Serenades, old fashioned waltzes, and, of course the mushy and sentimental songs, such as "Somewhere in France", that were inevitably thrown up by the war. Around midnight, when it finished, we danced rather than walked our way home, and Ted brought the house down when he thoughtlessly sang one of our army songs – "When this lousy war is over", the last line of which is well known to any soldier, and equally obvious to any civilian. He stopped suddenly, but too late, and his blush nearly cracked the black-out. Needless to say, fifty years on this 'gaffe' would not have raised an eyebrow!

One more leave highlight merits a mention – a Town Hall Ball, at which there appeared quite a large number of the local government employees who were serving in the 48th Div. Sigs. It was a splendid evening: floral decorations that made us gasp on entering the hall, a fine orchestra, quantities of good things to eat, and reunions with colleagues, many of whom we had not seen since the outbreak of war – some of them still in their old jobs, some in different branches of the services.

After this the sands of our embarkation leave drained rapidly away. When the day for departure came the central station, large as it was, overflowed with parents, wives, brothers, sisters and girl friends, seeing the 48th Div. Sigs. off to war. The contrast between our thoughts as we waved goodbye and those which had filled our heads but ten days earlier was stark indeed, and we were not well pleased when one of our more emotional comrades broke the long silence which followed the train's departure by articulating the thought that was in most of our minds: "I wonder how long it will be before we see them again?" For some of those in our compartment the answer was to be "More than five years".

I make no apology for dwelling at such length on this one, very special leave. For me, as for many of us, it marked a watershed: it was the end of the time when we had been little more than schoolboys in uniform, holding on as hard as we could to the values and habits of our life as civilians. On the other side of the divide there was to be increasing exposure to the reality of war-time soldiering, culminating in a climax beyond our wildest imaginings. For those of us who did return to England the war was by that time no longer the glorious open-air lark that it had seemed to many of us younger members of "Ack" Section, in those last few months of 1939.

Once back from leave, departure could not come too soon for most of us. True, the surrounding countryside, to which we had become so very attached, was looking lovelier than ever under a transforming mantle of snow. But equally true – it was very cold and there was no heating in the fowl pen! And we saw the snow in a rather different light after we had stood at attention in it for half an hour, waiting with freezing hands and feet for King George VI to inspect us – the reason for this somewhat dubious honour being that we were to be the first Territorial division to join the B.E.F. in France. I recall that in preparation for this occasion we had practised "cheering by numbers". I also recall that around this time I had welcomed the New Year by spending part of its first day on cookhouse fatigues and the rest – till 8p.m. – on packing up the officers' Mess furniture! On January 2nd a road party comprising around half our unit left with all our transport for the port of embarkation. With the roads like glass, those of us who were left behind were well content to make up the rail party which was to depart a week later.

When that day came, the march to the station was very different from that which had taken us off on leave less than three weeks earlier. With leaden feet and uncertain hearts we cursed to high heaven an army that got us from our beds at 3a.m. to catch a train that we knew would not depart till at least 10a.m. After interminable delays we trudged off to the Hungerford café where we were to have breakfast, dressed up once more, like Christmas trees; each one of us, as Clive so aptly put it, "a complete, mobile and self-contained unit of His Majesty's Fighting Forces". The final twist of the knife was that the café in which our breakfast had been ordered was the old favourite in which we had enjoyed many a double egg and chips.

The Southampton which eventually saw our train pulling in to its quayside on that miserable January day was a grey and sullen place. There followed long waits in best army style – on platforms, on quaysides, in road-ways – before we finally boarded the "Lady of Man". Once aboard the waiting continued. We waited for the boat to start moving; we waited in queues for the sandwiches and lemonade that were to be our day's rations; we went below decks and waited in the men's quarters, where we dozed off before stirring uneasily when the engines finally started up, in the small hours. After a few hours of fitful sleep dawn found most of us up on deck – drowsy and bad-tempered, but curious, and watching a grey sky gradually lightening to reveal the outline of what we took to be destroyers, escorting our small convoy. At about 10a.m. on January 9th we were slipping into Le Havre which, reservists apart, was for most of us our very first glimpse of "foreign parts".

Spirits rose as we watched fascinated, taking in the strangeness and novelty of it all – the different uniforms and clothing; the dockers who were truly shouting to one another in a language which up to that time had simply been a subject we had learned at school; the strange train which we rightly guessed was awaiting our arrival. But we were down to earth with a bump when our sergeant informed us that of all the 2,000 men on board the 30 or so who made up "Ack" Section had been selected to clean out the ship. We had cleaned out a fowl pen and a "Funk-hole"; we had cleaned out stables; on one occasion we had cleaned out a church! But a whole ship – ankle deep in cigarette packets, orange peel, and the like! Our complaining knew no bounds, and kept us so fully occupied that in a relatively short time the job was finished. The rest of the unit we found still waiting resignedly on the quayside, and shortly afterwards we all marched off across the dock to the nearby station, and boarded our train.

As if to bear out our stereotype of France and the French the train, when eventually it did set off, left half its carriages behind, stopped, reversed, joined them up again, and with much puffing and jolting was at last away – to where, we knew not. "Ack" Section was off to war!

Chapter 3

AT WAR IN FRANCE –
BEFORE THE BALLOON WENT UP

The train journey from the port to our first staging post in France – the little village of Yvetot, in Seine Inférieure – was strictly un-memorable. Our brief stay at Yvetot itself was another matter. It was here that we made our rendezvous with the road party which had left Chilton Foliat with our vehicles, 6 days ahead of us, and the excitement of this reunion knew no bounds. The British soldier needs only a few hours in a place to master all the true essentials, and the road party which had preceded us into Yvetot proved no exception. Of our group of five school friends, Phil – who had quickly become an extremely competent driver – had been a member of that advance guard and, like the rest of them, showed all the expected easy familiarity and proprietorship towards Yvetot and what it had to offer! Telling us that the cafés were open all day long, in no time at all he had us across the road in "our café". Addressing the buxom French lass behind the counter by her name, he ordered champagne – saying that he knew we would have to try it, because "at first" everyone was tickled by the novelty of champagne at around three shillings a bottle. Personally, he was tired of it, and preferred vermouth cassis.

There followed a night indeed. French drinks, at the equivalent of about two pence a glass, seemed unbelievably cheap to men brought up in a stern land where the cost of living was around a shilling a pint, and we quickly resolved to try every bottle on the café's display shelf. I believe I achieved this, but as the evening wore on one's assessment of the situation grew a little more hazy and there was a distinct tendency for the bottles to merge and then dance apart. Clive, who had been deputed to keep the score, produced the next day a scruffy, liquor-stained piece of paper that showed us to have consumed 23 drinks of 11 different varieties. Retribution, of course, was as swift as it was inevitable. We were ill, incredibly ill, and 0200 hours found all five of us – plus not a few others – out of our beds, spewing a violent, glittering green, which one felt would have exploded had a match been lit within yards of it. My head was bursting, my mouth felt as if it had been washed out with creosote, and I was very, very sorry for myself. I recorded at the time that such a monumental binge could only have resulted from a conspiracy between Satan and the Temperance movement, and it is certainly a fact that for the rest of my time in France I never drank anything but rum, (for warmth) or beer. A harsh experience that hangover may have been, but on balance, a pretty salutary one for a nineteen year old.

Next day, as the effects wore off, I began to take note of my surroundings. We were sleeping in an empty Salle des Fêtes – a sort of rudimentary theatre-cum-dance hall – and the first of several such billets that we were to come to know during the next few months. There was straw to lie on, and as one of the occupants of a sort of box, on the balcony, I was even protected from the worst of the draughts. In a yard at the back was to be found the inevitable French pump (frozen), and pervading the atmosphere was the equally inevitable odour of an imperfect sewage system. I spoke my first French, in a barber's shop, and I sent home a field postcard announcing my safe arrival. It was bitterly, bitterly cold.

Two more days and the journey to our final destination was resumed. This time it was to be by road, and in our Section's own vehicles. That journey is permanently etched in my memory, for its sheer, cruel agony. It was cold as we had never known cold before, and it introduced us to what was to be the coldest French winter in living memory – with 49 degrees of frost recorded at one stage – and the coldest within all of Europe for 50 years. The straight, unhedged roads seemed to reflect the frost back at us, and the very air seemed frozen.

The cold went straight through overcoat, battle-dress, scarves, pullovers and vests, striking as if with a sharp knife, into our very bones. Frequent halts were essential, to give us an opportunity to run around and get a little life back into numbed hands and feet; short as these breaks were, it was essential to keep the engines of our vehicles running all the time, if radiators were not to become blocks of ice. That the drivers stuck it out, perched for hour after hour, in the open, unprotected fronts of the horse-box like gin-palaces, seemed little short of a miracle. On the first of the two days of this final stage of our journey we covered only 80 miles, but it was more than enough. When we finally stopped for the night we experienced for ourselves the cold-weather drill for the vehicles that Phil, as a member of the road party, had already described to us. If anti-freeze had been invented by that time, the army certainly did not use it, and every evening the radiators of all vehicles were drained off, with engines still running. All through the night those on guard spent their shifts starting each truck's engine in turn, leaving them on to run for a time, and then switching off. Shortly afterwards the whole process would be repeated, and in this way the night would pass until the time came to re-fill radiators for the next day's journey. If any water was spilled at the filling, it would freeze on the front of the radiator. "Starting the engine", it should be said, was by swinging – it seemed interminably – a heavy starting handle, and it also needs to be said that quite often the attempt to start up a vehicle was completely unsuccessful. The sight of our 'motorised' unit on the move from the port – and, of course, all the other 48th Divisional units – with what looked like one half of the vehicles being towed by the other half, could not, I always felt, have done a great deal to inspire French confidence in their British allies!

Our convoy made a second and final overnight stop before arriving at our allocated "battle station". Influenced, no doubt by the arctic weather conditions, I described the small village in question as "typically French, dreary, drab and uninteresting". The five of us, inevitably, were caught for sentry duty at the vehicle park, but once that was over we set out to explore what our "dreary, drab and uninteresting" village had to offer. Five hearts lifted at the sight of a fair sized café, and five minds simultaneously registered "Egg and chips", but our high expectations were dashed the moment we were near enough to read the notice on the door: "Officers Only". Black rage, bitterness, hearty cursing. Before long, however, we had found a more than adequate substitute: a small, and, to British eyes, rather scruffy café, but one which was friendly and full of atmosphere, In no time at all we were enjoying our first decent meal since arriving in France, and – blessing of all blessings – a wash and shave in hot water. It was at least 48 hours since we had washed, and still longer since we had shaved, as of course all the water pumps encountered on our journey up to that point had been frozen solid.

On to a more thickly populated and industrial part of France, where one township seemed to run into the next. Strange to eyes that had never seen even a British mining district were the recurrent huge pyramids of pit spoil, and a sky obscured by a haze of coal-dust. Fascinating in a slightly grim sort of way were the first oblique and silent reminders of what we ourselves were doing there – beautifully kept war cemeteries, and overgrown trenches, shell-holes and dug-outs, left untouched since the end of our fathers' war. Our ultimate destination – Hénin Liétard – was a sizeable mining town, and arriving as we did, early on Saturday afternoon, we found it full of miners coming home from the pits – black faced and swinging their head-protecting helmets, each with his small barrel-like container of wine. A few read newspapers as they walked, but most were chatting away expressively to one another; in fact much the same as any group of British workers, always a little more animated than usual by Saturday dinner-time, with the prospect of a free weekend ahead of them.

All of this was very much to our liking. Certainly many of us had delighted in Chilton Foliat's fair countryside in those early months of the war, but French countryside – as experienced on the journey from the port – was another matter. Above all, perhaps, most of us were full of curiosity about the fabled, famous – and slightly fearsome – French gaiety and night life; and this, we thought, would surely be found only in a large town or city.

Before this could be put to the test, however, the usual routine of settling into a new location had to be accomplished. Once more we were in a concert hall, and this time it was situated behind a café-cum-barber's shop, off a rather grim and mean street in Montigny-en-Gohelle, on the outskirts of Hénin-Liétard. Our group of five school friends – Geoff, Phil, Clive, Maurice and myself – all together, as usual, had located ourselves on the stage of our concert hall billet, thinking – quite rightly – that the few stage props might furnish a little shelter from the draughts that would undoubtedly sweep through the large hall. By now we had acquired in good measure the soldier's aptitude for making himself as comfortable as possible, our eyes quick to notice nails convenient for hanging up kit, shelves to hold toilet articles, and the like. By this time, too, it was second nature for us to be kit conscious, to keep around us and jealously guard all our possessions, whether on a railway station, in the back of a lorry, or in a French billet.

Our first evening was given over to letter-writing, and our poor officers, getting their first taste of censoring, must have suffered indeed, as we all set to and poured out first impressions of France to relations and friends back home. For our part, though at first always conscious that other eyes than those of the addressees would be reading what we had written, all but the most self-conscious of us very quickly reached the stage of writing as if the censoring officer did not exist. And of course – as the ever practical Harry Sargeant soon realised and pointed out – a letter which the section officer would have to read was a near-perfect vehicle for a complaint or grouse of any sort that one wanted to bring to his attention!

Our first full day at Hénin was a Sunday, and after a morning and afternoon full of fatigues we prepared for a first, eagerly anticipated taste of the liberal French attitude towards the Sabbath: there were actually Sunday evening *dances* in Hénin, and we had every intention of attending one of them! It was an amazing experience. Admission was one franc – (the equivalent of about 1½ pence of the 1940 vintage, or just over one 'new' penny), and once past the entrance I immediately made my own small impact on the situation by going to a cloak room which opened onto the dance floor, taking off my size ten army boots, changing into the light-weight dancing shoes that most young soldiers regarded as a standard part of their war-time equipment, and depositing the boots with the cloak room attendant. This procedure – routine in any British dance hall – stopped the local French youths in their tracks, but it has to be said that their incredulity was more than matched by our own, when we looked around us. To start with, there was the matter of dress: Sunday best, for the men, seemed typically to be baggy trousers and loose jackets, violent coloured shirts and sandals. All of this was topped by hair that to our eyes seemed very long, together with very shapely sideboards. The generous use of perfume rounded off an impression that to conservative British youths seemed distinctly un-masculine! Then there was the dancing itself, and the music! Very different, it was, from our accustomed waltzes, quick-steps and slow foxtrots. The accordion was prominent, and the rhythm running through each and every tune seemed to us monotonously the same, calling for a continuous turning round and around, accompanied by an equally continuous bobbing up and down: "that continental music we hear on the wireless", as I described it in a letter home.

As the evening progressed the dance became increasingly lively, more and more crowded, and unbelievably noisy. At the heart of all the fun was a party of perhaps 20 young Frenchmen, newly conscripted and making the most of a final night out before the army swallowed them up. Most of them had coloured and decorated their faces, in some cases with highly realistic beards and moustaches; the liquor flowed freely, and they became more and more excited. Eventually, all eyes were on them as they danced together in pairs, before finally forming into a line and dancing snake-like, round the room, roaring out the famous and traditional 'Madelon'.

If the young men at the dance were something of a surprise to us, most of the girls were all that we hoped and expected they would be – beautifully groomed, charming, and very feminine. They clearly took a good view of the British soldiery, we felt sure we were doing fine, and we all had a splendid evening. At the end of the dance, as would have been the case in Britain, it seemed not unreasonable to suggest to our partners that perhaps they might like to be escorted home. The response was pretty well uniform: "Ah, non. Je suis avec maman", and one then became aware of what had been vaguely realised all the evening: that seated along each side of the room was a row of elderly battle-axes. Their role, as it seemed to us, was to watch their daughters like hawks, and ensure that they didn't repeat the same sort of fun that they themselves had enjoyed during the previous war. This first encounter with the French chaperoning system was, to say the least, highly educational, if not a little frustrating.

Educational in a different way was the encounter during a break at the bar with a friendly French airman, home on leave. We listened agog to his account of bringing down a German plane on Christmas Day; and when other French service-men joined in the ensuing discussion about the war in general we rapidly gained the impression that French soldiers were "red-hot" at their jobs and that they didn't think much of what they had so far experienced of the British army, although they did have a great respect for our navy and air force. All in all, a most enlightening evening – even if the reality of French night life, as lived in Hénin Liétard was somewhat different from the gay and romantic stereotype which prevailed at that time in Britain!

That we were out and about at all within such a short time of our arrival says much for the curiosity and zest for new experience of the young men of "Ack" Section, for the bitter cold of our journey to Hénin seemed to intensify with each successive day. One of my father's 1914–18 wartime stories, of which I had always been more than sceptical, was of cold so great that even the bread froze; but its truth was very swiftly borne out by our own experience in January 1940. And not just the bread! My hair froze if I put through it a comb which had been dipped in water. Harry Sargeant reported in a letter to his wife that his cap had literally frozen on his head; and on another occasion, that after a wash under a tap, the water froze on his face until he nearly cried with pain. The contents of our water bottles froze solid at night, only a foot or so from bed spaces. One evening, when walking into Hénin, sleet fell, our greatcoats were swiftly frozen solid as boards, and were as difficult to take off as the armour of a knight of old. Balaclava helmets became the most appreciated of all the comforts for the troops and were worn at all times. We ate, and we slept, in every article of clothing we could get on. Socks would be frozen stiff by morning if they were inadvertently taken off and left out side the bed. With only 2 blankets per man we would pool resources and huddle 3 – sometimes even 4 – in a bed (on the bare boards of the floor, of course). If a measure of the impact of these appalling conditions were needed it would probably be difficult to improve on the comment of one of our number, in a letter home that read, "Sgt. Gattrell has got awful chilblains and has been walking about in pumps in this terrible cold. He has been very miserable and I feel sorry for him, even though he is a sergeant". But unbelievably grim as it undoubtedly was, I think we would all have agreed that what we suffered did not begin to compare with the winters in the trenches, that characterised our fathers' war.

For us, the real life-saver at this time was rum – often diluted in a bowl of hot water, when it was known as 'grog'. Once in a while there would be an official issue – "when the great ones think about it" as we would occasionally comment with some bitterness – but more often it would be purchased as needed, from the café in front of our billet, blatantly ignoring the regulations which restricted the British troops' access to estaminets and cafés to the hours of 12–2p.m. and 6–9.30p.m. One particularly vivid memory of this time is of the kindness of a local French house-wife when we were engaged in what was probably the most miserable of all the fatigues inflicted upon us during that dreadful winter. With ground frozen so hard and so deep that effective penetration really called for a pneumatic drill, we were ordered to dig, with picks and shovels, the latrine to end all latrines – 10 feet long, 2 feet wide and 8 feet deep! The task took its profane course, over a period of some days, and all the time we were kept going by jugs of scalding hot coffee from the good lady in question. The final irony, so typical of the army, was that the latrine was scarcely completed before we were ordered to fill it in again: it seemed that we had mistakenly been billeted outside our Corps area, and we were to move to a new location at Dourges, a few miles away!

By that time we were already becoming familiar with the ways of the French and with France – or at least, our little bit of it. We would congregate in the little café in front of our billet, which always had a good fire, and exchange badinage with the proprietor – a huge man, who looked a proper tough – and his two daughters. The younger, about 12 years of age, was plump, fair, and doll-like, and made much of by the soldiery. The elder, Annette, was about 17 and quite attractive, and all the troops tried to flirt with her. The unit which had preceded us in this locality had taught her a few of the simpler English phrases. She would say "No damn good" with a pretty French accent and loved to embarrass the shyer members of the section by saying "Kees me" – while making sure they had no opportunity to do so; or "Bootiful Jeem", (or "Frankie", or "Mo-rees", as the case may be). One or two of the reservists, after regarding her ample figure with knowledgeable eyes, asserted that a basic knowledge of their language was pretty certainly not the only thing the departed English soldiers had left with her!

Our general impression of the French was that they were well disposed towards us, and friendly enough, but it was pretty clear that they found it irritating to say the least, that our call-up in Britain extended at that time only to 26 or 27 year-olds, while in France they were already calling up men well into their forties. With hindsight it was pretty clear that pinpricks such as these contributed to French apathy and lack of resolution in the face of events to come. Certainly the German propaganda machine played skilfully on such matters, and when, one night, leaflets were dropped telling the citizens of Hénin that their soldiers were up in the Maginot line at a franc a day – fighting for English capitalism – while the plutocratic English troops were seducing French soldiers' wives, in the back area, the propaganda fell on very receptive ears.

Our move to the adjacent mining village of Dourges was to bring us into much closer contact with the local population – many of whom were of Polish origin, having settled in the area around the time of the

first World War. A popular café with many of us was in fact the Café
Polski, and before long our relationship with its habitués was confirmed
and cemented by a football match in which, although Clive had spread
it around that Geoff was an international and three other members of
our team played for Arsenal, we were well and truly trounced. Probably
our favourite café, however, was the one we referred to as the Café of
the Brunette – the brunette being an extremely attractive young lady
named Juanita. A further point in its favour was that it offered bar
billiards, a game at which we soon became very proficient; and
furthermore we could even pick up Henry Hall's Guest Night on the
café's wireless set. At a somewhat loftier level Ken Boodson, one of my
librarian colleagues, managed one night to talk the proprietor into
allowing him to listen to Beethoven on the wireless set in the kitchen!
Juanita, however, was undoubtedly the main attraction, but a watchful
aunt and Juanita's own inbuilt modesty and discretion ensured that the
attention of the troops never progressed beyond silent – sometimes not
so silent – admiration during the café's working hours. A memory that
stays with me still is that of a splendid "poor ignorant male" act by Clive
– ever the optimist – in which he spent the best part of an evening
ostentatiously and unsuccessfully attempting to sew a button on his
uniform – a ploy which left Juanita completely unmoved!

The married men amongst us were more inclined to seek out
"home comforts", and before many weeks had passed two of my fellow
librarians – Ken Boodson and Harry Sargeant – had established a very
happy relationship with a local mining family, in whose home they
passed many an evening, and consumed many an "egg and chips".
Nearly 50 years later Harry, Clive, Phil and I were to re-visit that family,
and find the three children of 1940, by that time, had become middle
aged to elderly citizens with families of their own, and Bambette the
dog and Archambaud, the cat, alas no more than a memory.

On Sunday it was not uncommon for local miners to entertain their
British allies in truly French style, with a repast of snails washed down
by the local 'fire-water', and we became accustomed on such occasions
to the arrival in the billet of a beaming, singing group of "A" Section

members, reeking of garlic and more than a "peu Zig-Zag"! After one such party the tongue of Slim Ryder, one of our reservists, was loosened to such good effect that for the best part of an hour he held us spell-bound as he progressed systematically round the entire billet, pointing out to each and every one of us, with disconcertingly perceptive and completely uninhibited frankness, our strong and weak points – particularly the latter.

An evening with the miners had, however, the opposite effect on one of our group of 5 school friends. He went straight to his bed, without a word, and fully dressed, and defied all my efforts to wake him, some 4 hours later, when he was due to relieve me on wireless watch – of which more shortly. That night I did a double watch.

That hospitality was a strong trait with the miners of Dourges, there could be no doubt, but an equally strong characteristic was their love of gambling – particularly in connection with a sport to which many of them were fanatically addicted – cock-fighting. These engagements took place on Sunday afternoons, and during peace time there was a regular circuit of villages which hosted them. Hearing that a fight was to take place locally, we decided to broaden our experience by a visit to it – and "broadening" it certainly was! Visualize a small area with tiers of benches all round, thronged with as many of the local population as could squeeze in – men, women, children and babies alike. Such is the scene when the fight is due to begin, but for a good hour before this, preliminary side shows outside the building have been keeping the crowd amused. Crown and anchor was particularly well patronised, card tricks were performed, groups sat around gambling, and the whole area buzzed with activity.

Certain Sunday-best clad miners with sacks under their arms, and an air at once self conscious and proprietary, turned out to be the owners of the gladiators who were to perform for us. When the show was declared open, a sort of 'Maître d'Affaires' announced the names of the two birds which were to start proceedings, and their owners. Each bird was equipped with vicious, needle-like spurs, and the moment they were released they got straight down to business. No circling and sparring for openings: each fled squawking, straight at its opponent; feathers flew, blood flowed, and the audience wound itself up to fever pitch, with side-bets flying fast and furious as each bird strove for the kill. Once a bird was down its opponent would place a spur-clad claw on its neck and begin to peck away viciously. In a two hour performance 3 or 4 birds were killed, and several badly hurt. Failing a kill it was considered a defeat if a bird was down for three minutes. Though not without a certain gruesome fascination, cock-fighting struck most of us as a pretty dreadful business, and an experience which we had no wish to repeat.

A rather more civilised aspect of the French Sunday, and one which never ceased to attract us, was the parade of all the locals in their Sunday best. In the words of Harry Sargeant, reporting to his wife in England "On Sundays and fête days they don't half deck themselves up: men in bell-bottomed bags, fancy waistcoats and bowlers, women in all sorts of posh outfits. Smart as paint. Babies come out in superb woolly coats and whatnots, with ribbons in their hair".

Yet another fascinating facet of French life was to be found much nearer home. The concert-hall in which we were billeted was in the very large "back yard" of a café on a side street of Dourges. Access was via a small door set into a huge pair of solid double doors next to the café, or alternatively through the café itself. In addition to the concert-hall, the back yard contained a fowl pen, the occupants of which spent most of their time "free-ranging" over the whole area, two cows who never left a tiny cow shed, which included a special cow-latrine that was pumped out from time to time, to the accompaniment of a vile smell; a pigsty which seemed to have been built around a single occupant, who like the cows was never allowed out; the troops' latrine; our wash-place next to the pig-sty; a huge heap of steaming manure; a forge and a blacksmith's shop. Pottering about the yard, or sitting on a chair inside the café was nearly always to be seen an ancient who was clearly the head of the whole clan, and reputed to remember the days of the 1870 conflict with the "Sale Boches". He was possessed of a single conversational phrase which he used on every possible occasion: "Fait froid, huh?"

Here on our doorstep, in Dourges, was this fascinating combination of urban and rural France, as manifest in a small village which effectively was absorbed in quite a large town – Hénin-Liétard. Very quickly we came to terms with the new and strange environment represented by the café-cum small holding on which we were billeted – just as we had come to terms with Chilton Foliat's fowl pen. Very swiftly we were turning the situation to our advantage – in fact to the mutual advantage of the French proprietors and ourselves – for the café enjoyed a liberal supply of eggs from its back-yard hen-run, and our own unvarying breakfast ration comprised a rasher of bacon, delivered each morning by the Company's cooks. Such a combination spelled a regular breakfast of two eggs and bacon, taken in the café, and swilled down, of course, by mugs of army tea. This notwithstanding, it has to be said that army diet in general was pretty dull, and Clive one day indulged in a little quantification which revealed that if leave was 150 days away, during that time an "A" Section soldier would have consumed 150 pieces of bacon between 300 slices of bread, 75 stews, 75 roasts, 300 pieces of toast and 75 gallons of tea. Let it not be thought, however, that this truly represented the full range of our diet. In Britain rationing had still to bite very deeply, and most of us received a steady flow of parcels from home in which food figured prominently; and in addition of course, there was always on sale the magnificent French patisserie, the like of which few of us had ever experienced before.

The first few months of 1940, then, saw "A" Section adjusting to and coming to terms with a new and very different environment – and doing it, during the early weeks, in unremittingly arctic-like conditions. Before long training of a sort got under way. A lecture on a new gas, arsene, which was both odourless and invisible, left us depressed and somewhat anxious, though we did in fact receive a special new fitment for our gasmasks, which was alleged to cope with it. An Easter Sunday spent on the rifle range – up to our knees in mud – confirmed that shooting practice in France was just as unspeakably wretched a way of spending time as it had been in England. Route marches, likewise, followed the Chilton Foliat pattern – as soon as we were out of sight of the powers that be, the old-soldier in charge of us would fall out the column to smoke, gossip, and spend the time in any way other than hardening our feet and leg muscles. A trial move-out, early in March, seemed a little more to the point, especially as it gave us one of our first sights of the sun since arriving in France: in fact, having arrived at our destination, we spent the whole afternoon playing cards in the open air, at the side of our truck, concluding with a picnic tea from our parcels-from-home provisions. Returning after dark, in convoy, provided an extra and unplanned element of training, for down one very narrow lane we found Ken Rider's wireless truck well and truly ditched, and keeling over at a very precarious angle – the consequences of over-taking in the dark. On the instruction of attendant redcaps (Military Police) and an officer from an L.A.D. (Light Aid Detachment) we towed him out, the risk of his overturning while we did so, on account of the angle at which he was ditched, being counteracted by pressure from a whole group of assembled soldiery on the lower side of his vehicle.

One of the most effective means of training, and one which we all appreciated because it was concerned with authentic problems of the sort that were more than likely to confront us, was a series of lectures from our old soldiers – the reservists; we could have done with more of these. But for us, as a wireless section, probably the most useful training of all was "press watch" and "listening watch". Within a very short time of our arrival in France our Section was made responsible for recording the news sent out in Morse code, in the English language, by organisations such as Reuters. Three teams of two, each made up of one reservist and one Territorial, covered the whole night between them, and Geoff, Phil and I counted ourselves as very fortunate to be the first 3 of our Territorials to benefit in this way. In the early weeks, when the cold was at its most intense, the canvas-covered wireless vehicle in which we carried out our watch was not the most comfortable place in which to pass the small hours, but there was compensation in the form of a spell of excused duty during the day-time. Most importantly of all, however, was the fact that there was obvious point and purpose in what we were doing. The end-product of our night's activities was a news-sheet which was intended for the Division's top brass, and which also appeared in the Officers' Mess at breakfast time each morning. All of this was extremely good for our Morse speeds: in no time at all I was comfortably receiving twenty words a minute, and for short spells very considerably more; though once again, this speed in receiving was substantially in excess of that at which one could confidently transmit. To press watch there was shortly to be added a variant in the form of listening watch – listening for German stations, normally transmitting in code, and taking down what they were sending. As the content was naturally completely unintelligible this was in some ways much duller than press watch, and we never learned what value, if any, attached to what we had intercepted; but at least it seemed to provide a tiny scrap of involvement – however marginal – in the war of which we were supposed to be a part; and identifying coded messages, often disentangling them from heavy atmospherics, could only be good for our Morse.

Let it not be thought, however, that training was allowed to get in the way of the fatigues which from the beginning had been a major element in our lives as soldiers of the King. France, in fact, was to enlarge and enrich our experience in ways that were certainly unexpected and, equally certainly, were covered in none of the standard military handbooks! For example, the long arm of Montigny-en-Gohelle, where we were wrongly located before moving to Dourges, and the scene of our famous 8ft x 10ft x 2ft latrine, reached out to us again in early March: it seemed that what we thought was waste ground, in which we had buried our Section's enormous accumulation of tins and other rubbish, was in fact someone's allotment, and in the interests of Anglo/French harmony we were detailed to dig the whole lot out again, and bury it elsewhere. Even less pleasant was a job which came Harry Sargeant's way: the clearing up of various rubbish heaps in the back yard in which our Dourges billet was situated – including one pile which consisted of human excrement – and combining them in one big heap next to the food stores! Then there was the gloriously sunny Saturday when Geoff, Phil and I were caught for a job which required us to build a cookhouse oven. There were bricks – old bricks – but no materials for mortar; the sergeant's response when we hopefully pointed this out to him was "Well, use *!# mud, then". So we did. Rather more satisfying was a task for which Geoff and I were detailed and which we succeeded in spreading out over a full week. It was to build a portable latrine, and we made a very fine job of it indeed. It was an affair of about six feet in length, in wood, with four carefully smoothed and rounded holes in the top, four lids, each hinged with leather, and sliding under each of them, from the back, was one of the multi-purpose, square sectioned four gallon petrol tins, minus its top. The pièce de résistance was a strip of beading at the end, which, we thought, finished off the job very nicely! This portable latrine became our Section's pride and joy, and we were to feel many a pang at the thought that in due time it was undoubtedly taken into use by the Germans.

Far less acceptable were fatigues such as coal shovelling and scrubbing out officers' billets – only to find that when we had done so they had changed their minds about which rooms they would use, because of the possibility of draughts. As in Chilton Foliat, and with equally good reason, our group of school friends continued to get more than a fair share of all the fatigues that were going, and eventually Clive was moved to produce a large notice which we attached to the wall behind the area in which our five bed spaces were located. The fact that only four of our names are mentioned on it was due to the fact that Maurice Brett had decided to opt for the life of a driver-batman, which exempted him from all fatigues. The notice is shown on the next page.

Even the officer laughed when he saw this notice. The sergeant, however, did not think it was so very funny!

Badly as we felt at times about the number of fatigues that came our way, it has to be admitted that we had a fair amount of free time, particularly in the evenings, and that there was no real shortage of pleasant ways of filling it. A walk of about a mile and a half would take us to Hénin with its cafés and patisseries – and, even more important, a frequently changing programme of films specially brought over for the British troops. I recorded a total of 23 which I attended between January

A.S.P.T.I.I.

HAVE YOU

A

JOB

THAT WANTS DOING

APPLY TO:– 'A' Sect FATIGUES TRUST INC. LTD.

C. E. TOMRY SHOUT FOR

HIM THEN LOOK
ROUND FOR

ONE or ALL of:– P. M VANE

W L SAUNDERS

G F NEWMAN

ALL of WHOM HAVE LONG EXPERIENCE IN:–
SANITARY CONSTRUCTION AND
MAINTENANCE
BRICKLAYING
FOOD TRANSPORT
COOKHOUSE FATIGUES
HAULAGE
EXCAVATING
SHIP CLEANERS
AND SLIGHT EXPERIENCE IN
WIRELESS OPERATING
SOLDIERING

SATURDAYS, SUNDAYS AND NIGHTTIME A
SPECIALITY.
«WE WORK WHILE OTHERS REST».

and April, ranging from Dorothy Lamour's Her Jungle Lover to The Plainsman; from Wells Fargo to The Thin Man; from Gracie Field in "We're going to be rich" to Marlene Dietrich in The Scarlet Emperor. Then there were N.A.A.F.I. concerts, and occasionally, personal appearances of 'big names' such as Leslie Henson, Gracie Fields, Arthur Askey, Jack Hylton and many others; though for these there was usually only a limited number of tickets, for which we drew lots. If we decided to spend the evening in our billet we could always read and, like many others, I received a steady flow of books – mostly Penguins and Pelicans – from home: looking at the titles I read in this way I could wish that my reading in later years had always been as extensive, and at such a respectable level, as during those few months in France. Before long, too, our billet had its own wireless set, which we hired for a sum that called for a contribution of threepence a week from each of us; on this we could pick up programmes from Britain that ranged from Vera Lynn singing "Somewhere in France with you" to classical music – the only problem being to gain unanimity amongst all who wished to listen. One of our section officers, who had been a school master, did his best to provide an educational alternative for those whose inclinations ran in that direction. There were, for instance, French lessons, and an evening debating session. Of the latter, Harry Sargeant was appointed Secretary, and recorded the fact that no-one at all turned up for the first meeting, all the troops having cleared off down town. Shades of the later years of the war, and A.B.C.A.! (Army Bureau of Current Affairs).

Then, of course there was always gambling. I still think with some incredulity of the hours and hours that I spent in this way – as, indeed did many other members of our Section – and would only say that it got gambling out of my system completely, for good and all. My record of gains and losses – principally the latter – ranged from 7 francs to as much as 100 francs; 'brag' was the favourite, but there are frequent entries for crown and anchor, pontoon and housey housey. One hilarious recollection is of a not particularly popular sergeant coming into the billet one day to check on those of our number who were in their beds, excused duty as sufferers from a 'flu' epidemic that was going the rounds, and finding several of the invalids, including Maurice and Phil, indulging in a nice session of housey housey. Crown and Anchor, for some reason which was never really clear to me, was regarded by the army authorities as just about the ultimate in depravity, and according to reservist folk-lore carried really extreme penalties for those – usually 'old sweats' – who owned the boards and ran the sessions. The 'boards' in fact were usually made of cloth or oil skin, and their owners would produce them from under their battle dress jackets with conjurer-like deftness, if the occasion seemed right – and could make them disappear with equal speed if 'authority' hove into sight. There was an elaborate and traditional ritual of patter from the "Nobby" who ran a crown and anchor board. As recorded by my fellow librarian, Harry Sargeant it went something like this: "Who's for a go on the old dicky die doh, gents; N.C.O.s orderly officers and brigade majors play this game; plonk it down thick and heavy, the more you put down the more you pick up – a nice bet to you sir – 20 francs on the old mud-hook [i.e. anchor] and 10 on the major [i.e. crown] – a nice bet to you sir – 5 on the dicky die doh and one on the gravedigger – who's for the heart and club – nice bet to you sir – lay your bets gents, you come here in barrows and go away in coaches, silks and satins of the orient – any more before she goes over – all finished gents – orderly officers play this game – up she goes gents up she comes – 2 hearts on dicky die doh – Nobby's all right this time, gents, Nobby's all right this time (raking in the cash); wait until the board's clear before laying your bets, gents. etc., etc."

This wide range of spare-time activities notwithstanding, it is a fact that these early months with the B.E.F. in France were characterised for most of us by acute and frequent attacks of home-sickness and there were few of our number who did not spend a fair bit of time thumbing through the collections of photographs of wives, girl friends, parents, brothers, sisters, and in some cases children, which pretty well all soldiers carried in their wallets. Harry Sargeant, who had a splendid gift for verbalising sentiments and situations of all sorts, recorded in a letter to his wife the substance of his evening "hate" (there being 3 such "hate" sessions each day – morning, post-prandial, and evening). It reads as follows:

"Curse all the armed forces of every nation, army, navy, and airforce, A.R.P., civil service, local and central government, A.F.S., W.A.T.S., W.A.A.F.S., Girl Guides, Life Brigades, Scouts, Cubs and Brownies, L.D.V.'s, Home Guards, M.P.'s, Dictators, Presidents, Kings and countries that keep me separated from my wife, with particular reference to the 48th Divisional Signals and with significant and detailed application to Major 'Good, Splendid, Excellent' Jones and Captain Carping King and Lieut. Loopy Liddington and their ilk: and I hope they all read this. The men have already fallen out and are cleaning their vehicle engines by the light of glow worms collected by a fatigue party from Scotland, until the officers get back from B Mess". This particular example of an evening "hate" nicely encapsulates the feelings that beset most of us from time to time during those early months with the B.E.F.

Another manifestation of home-sickness was the amount of our spare time that we devoted to letter writing: this must of course have been a sore trial to our officers, whose duties included reading and censoring all outgoing mail. Incoming mail, at this early stage, was an absolutely essential life-line, and I recently re-read with some incredulity a diary entry for late January 1940, in which I was expressing great anxiety that I had not heard from home since the previous Sunday: the entry was made on Thursday!

It was significant too that the long and animated discussions in which we engaged – whether in our billet, in the evening, or walking into Hénin – tended always to be about the past or the future. Geoff and I, for example, would retrace mile by mile the glorious walking holidays we had spent in Devonshire and the Cotswolds; and the whole group of us, at the drop of a hat, would embark on truly animated discussions of plans for our post-war careers – even though we were beginning to realise that 'post-war' was likely to be a lot further away than had seemed likely during that first flush of excitement and optimism when we were mobilised, not so many months earlier.

Home-sickness, the intense cold, and the general atmosphere of 'phoney-war' which prevailed at that time posed a continuous challenge for those whose business it was to maintain the morale of our troops at

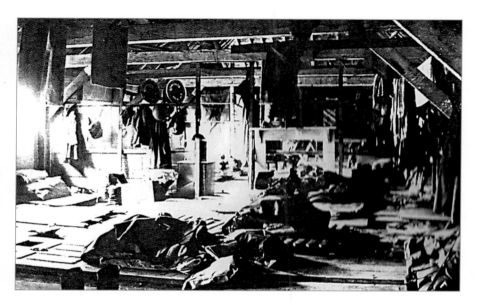

Interior view of 'Fowl Pen' Chilton Foliat, 1940.

Exterior view of 'Fowl Pen' Chilton Foliat, photograph 2004.

NOTHING is to be written on this side except the date and signature of the sender. Sentences not required may be erased. If anything else is added the post card will be destroyed.

[Postage must be prepaid on any letter or post card addressed to the sender of this card.]

I am quite well.

~~I have been admitted into hospital~~

{ ~~sick~~ } ~~and am going on well.~~
{ wounded } ~~and hope to be discharged soon.~~

~~I am being sent down to the base.~~

~~I have received your~~ { ~~letter dated~~ _____
{ ~~telegram~~ ,, _____
{ ~~parcel~~ ,, _____

Letter follows at first opportunity.

~~I have received no letter from you~~

{ ~~lately~~
{ ~~for a long time.~~

Signature only } *Will*

Date _9th Jan. 1940._

Forms /A 2042 /7.   51-4997.

Standard Army letter sent back when arrived in France Jan 9th 1940.

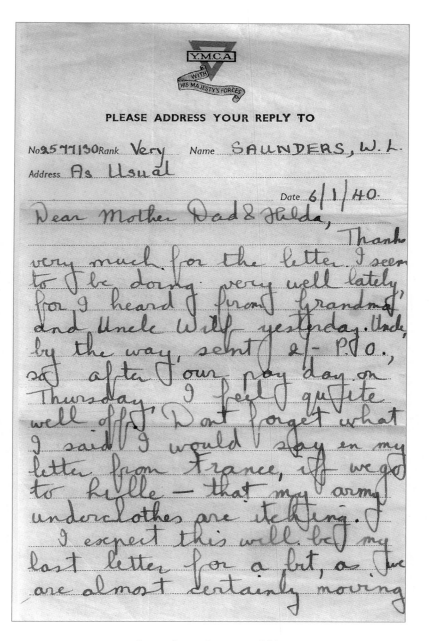

PLEASE ADDRESS YOUR REPLY TO

No. 2577130 Rank Very   Name SAUNDERS, W. L.
Address As Usual

Date 6/1/40.

Dear Mother Dad & Hilda,

Thank very much for the letter. I seem to be doing very well lately, for I heard from Grandma and Uncle Will yesterday. Uncle, by the way, sent 2/- P.O., so after our pay day on Thursday I feel quite well off. Don't forget what I said I would say in my letter from France, if we go to hille — that my army underclothes are itching.

I expect this will be my last letter for a bit, as we are almost certainly moving

Letter home (see page 38).

XI

TO THE GLORY OF GOD

AND IN MEMORY OF THE MEN
OF THE ROYAL WARWICKSHIRE REGIMENT
THE CHESHIRE REGIMENT
AND THE ROYAL ARTILLERY
WHO ON 28TH MAY 1940
WERE MASSACRED
IN A BARN NEAR THIS SPOT
ALSO OF THE MEN WHO WERE MURDERED
AS THEY WERE BEING MARCHED
TO THE BARN

WE WILL REMEMBER THEM...

THIS MEMORIAL
IS ERECTED BY THE BIRMINGHAM BRANCH
DUNKIRK VETERANS' ASSOCIATION

*Wormhout/Esquelbecq Memorial to the massacred
of the Royal Warwickshire Regiment.*

Telegram sent to parents from Alfreton on return to England after Dunkirk.

*Relaxation moment. Lofty Hines & Wilf Saunders in Lew Mill 1940.
Note rifles & kit around them.*

At ease outside 'Gin Palace', Wilf Saunders is second from right.

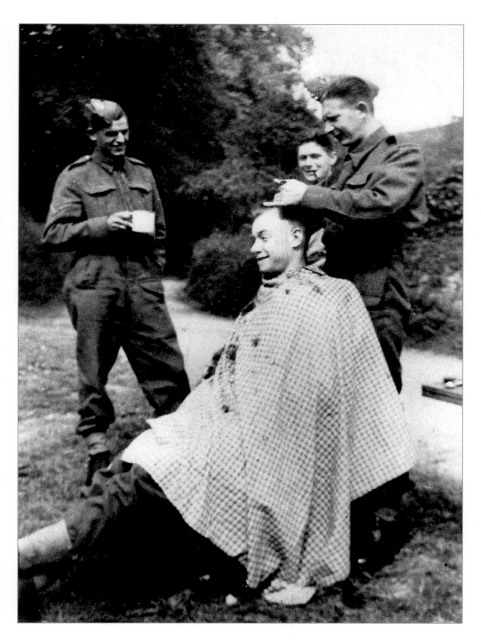

Ken Rider's first haircut after Dunkirk.

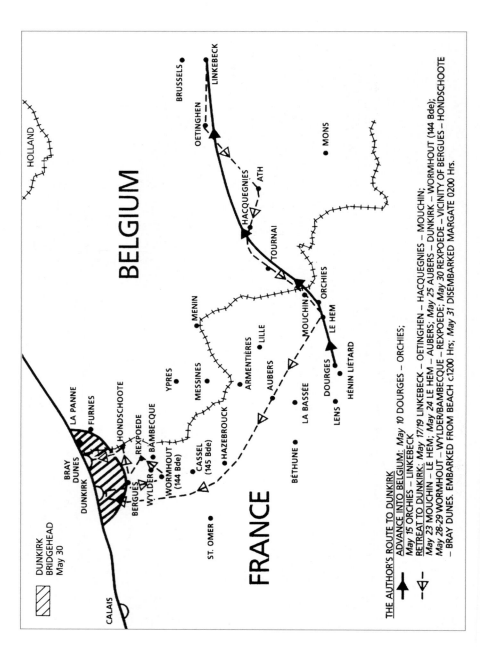

Map of Advance through France & Dunkirk Retreat.

a high level, and it has to be said that the pitch to which Montgomery raised the level of morale and training in his 3rd Division was very much the exception in the B.E.F. in France, in 1940. In our own unit the reservists, with many years of peace-time regular army soldiering behind them, could at times become very frustrated by the inadequacies of many of our Territorial officers and N.C.O.s, and were often extremely scathing in their criticism: sometimes, indeed, downright rebellious. On one occasion, early in February, the senior N.C.O. in charge of a parade of our Section announced that there would be a compulsory lecture on each of the following 3 days, between 5 and 6 o'clock in the evening – normally free time. Pandemonium broke loose. All the reservists present started to shout at once, led by a little Welshman who went into a continuous chant of "What a shower of *#+", while another old soldier was bawling out "I suppose it's Mr. Bleeding One-Star –" (one of our junior officers). The Territorial senior N.C.O. in charge seemed completely powerless to restore any semblance of order! I must say that for my own part I thought it hilarious, and creased up with laughter – but the fact is, of course, that such a situation high-lighted the inexperience and disciplinary weakness of some, at least, of the Territorial N.C.O.s.

Far more serious was the desertion into Belgium of two thoroughly frustrated and browned-off old soldiers from another company of our unit. Nearer home, around the same time, the word went around that one of the more volatile of our own 'Ack' Section reservists had become so fed up when a particularly ineffectual Territorial N.C.O. had unjustifiably put him on a charge, that he had cleared off with one of our vehicles, after trying unsuccessfully to persuade another reservist to desert with him to Belgium. The missing reservist was very popular with all of us, and we were very apprehensive for him, so that it was almost a relief when he turned up soon after midnight – very drunk, and in trouble – but with his truck intact: he had been found by one of our unit's officers in the throes of a monumental binge, with a friend. The price he paid for this escapade was 14 days field punishment, but if he had truly deserted, the punishment would have been far worse.

However, field punishment itself was fearsome enough. It no longer involved being fastened spread-eagled to a gun limber for several hours each day, as had been the case in World War 1, but an offender was worked flat out, for every waking hour, and everything he did had to be carried out at the double. This included hard physical labour such as filling sandbags, stone breaking, and the like, and a daily non-stop two hours of pack drill with full kit, presided over by a Military Policeman who could only be described as a proper bastard. After the pack drill he would put the prisoners through physical jerks until they dropped – literally, as we found out for ourselves when we saw two members of our own unit being subjected to this ordeal.

The announcement that home leave was to start in April – 10 days each – gave a very definite boost to morale, and of our group of school friends Geoff Newman was one of the lucky few to be drawn with the first batch. In the event, German military activities – notably the invasion of Norway and Denmark, of which more shortly – were to cause the repeated postponement of the original leave date, but Geoff finally did get away just before the invasion of the Low Countries put a complete end to home leave possibilities.

Good for morale, too, was the commencement of a system by which each of us was allowed a full day's pass on a Saturday or Sunday to the nearby metropolis of Lille. As signs of spring began to show themselves Lille seemed to our inexperienced eyes to be the ultimate in sophistication with its gay boulevards full of smartly dressed men and women, and cafés with seats overflowing onto the pavements, where one could sit and sip a drink while an orchestra played inside. The famous red-light district was of course a source of considerable fascination for young men from a relatively puritan Britain, and a visit was more or less mandatory. Quite apart from any question of morality, the effectiveness of the lectures we had received from our officers, on the dangers of V.D., and the gruesome nature of the treatment if one contracted it, ensured that for most of the younger soldiers, at least, a visit to one of these establishments never went beyond the purchasing of an extremely expensive drink and a feeling of very considerable embarrassment. I think it is fair to say that for most of the troops, eager to taste the fabled French "gaiety and nightlife", a visit to the red-light district of Lille was a pretty disillusioning experience!

Interestingly, one of the most important of all boosts to morale was provided by the continuing unfolding of the war itself. On April 9th our whole unit was to set out on the first real exercise since our arrival in France, our destination being a village called Rieux, not far from Abbeville. That very day, before we left Dourges, rumour had it that Norway and Denmark had been invaded, but we departed all the same and very soon were too busy admiring the beautiful countryside – so very different from Dourges and Hénin – to bother too much about the news. Once arrived we had time on our hands and opened up our wireless set in search of press transmissions. We soon gained confirmation of the invasion, and the news was very bad: the Danes had already surrendered, leaving the Germans free to concentrate on Norway. Against all expectations, our exercise, due to commence the next morning, was not cancelled, and that evening four of us took advantage of the free time to climb to the top of the highest hill in the neighbourhood, from where we saw a splendid sunset across an echoing valley, which was very reminiscent of our own Cotswolds. The stark contrast between the beauty of our surroundings and the news of events in Denmark and Norway came through very forcibly to all of us, and we returned to our trucks in sombre mood. Next morning, after a 5 o'clock reveille, the exercise duly started, but at 8 o'clock in the evening it was hurriedly cancelled, and after a tiring drive through the night we were back in Dourges at 4 o'clock the following morning. Here we were put under 2 hours notice to move. It was in fact the afternoon before our detachment got away – Clive and I were together, along with a young Territorial lance corporal, with one of our most experienced reservists, Arthur Hillier, as the corporal in charge. Our orders, which Arthur picked up from Divisional Headquarters, were to report to "A" Corps in Esquerchin, and it was thought that we would start work that night, probably as Directing Station on a Nine Set wireless link to French cavalry. During our journey Arthur gave us a very effective little homily, making the point that this was now real war and that we must obey him implicitly, but going on to express his complete confidence that we should all do a good job of work. This was the sort of talk, and Arthur's the sort of leadership that three raw youngsters needed, and responded to. I know that I myself felt a great glow of excitement – a sort of "Now we are really off – let's get at them" feeling; and I felt myself to be immensely fortunate to be starting 'war for real' with Arthur Hillier as my detachment commander.

What followed was in fact anti-climax of the sort that war and the army so often provide. On our arrival at Esquerchin there was no immediate operational role for us, and we were put on stand-by; and on stand-by we remained for the next 12 days! It was a tribute to Arthur Hillier that he managed to keep us up to the mark during this period – he gave us instruction in wireless theory, electricity and magnetism, operating procedures, and all sorts of miscellaneous military matters, and even whipped up enthusiasm for a thorough-going cleaning of our vehicle, inside, outside and underneath – a process that occupied two days and finished up with us all as black and oil-stained as seamen in a ship's engine room. In the background all the time, however, was fear: not of the war and the enemy, but of being caught for guard duty at Corps Headquarters, Esquerchin. Our first sight of this guard being mounted shook us to the core. Spit and polish as we had never seen it before: gleaming brass and boots, immaculately blanco-ed equipment, and a mounting drill of great complexity, executed with guardsman-like precision. The commanding officer, we were told, was an absolute martinet, whose approach was that "soldiering" definitely took priority over technical signals matters, with guard mounting drill occupying 3 full days of rehearsal before it actually happened! Days went by and we were left unmolested, but we were in constant fear that it could not last, and about a week after our arrival the blow fell: we were told we were likely to be permanently posted to "A" Corps. This meant without a shadow of doubt that our turn for guard duty would come, not to mention, of course, the fact that we would be separated from all our friends in "Ack" Section. This news was confirmed the next day by our Section Officer, who was visiting us.

Two days later a message arrived instructing us to pack up immediately and return to "Ack" Section at Dourges! As we were learning, in the army one needed to be prepared for anything.

Not only our detachment but the whole Section came pouring back to Dourges that day and there was great excitement and exchanging of experiences. My twentieth birthday had taken place during our absence, and though masses of cards and three huge parcels had been delivered to me at Esquerchin, I had deferred the celebration proper until our group of school friends was together again. The evening of our return provided the occasion: unlimited beer at the Café of the Brunette, and vast quantities of food – my parcels included two birthday cakes from Barrows (Birmingham's answer to Fortnum and Masons), sent to me by girls from the Library I had worked in before mobilisation, plus a cake with 20 candles from my elder sister, iced by her engineer husband. The most notable presents were a Rolls Razor from my family and Herbert Read's "Knapsack" – the best anthology for a soldier that has ever come my way – from my girl friend.

Maurice Brett's 20th birthday, like my own, had taken place during our absence from Dourges, and we made it a joint party, with his accumulation of birthday goodies being added to my own. The general pattern had already been set by Geoff Newman's 20th, just before the Danish/Norwegian flap, but in one important respect it was necessarily different: at 9 o'clock on the evening of Geoff's party we had drunk to his parents, back home, knowing that they were reciprocating at exactly that time. In the case of Maurice and myself the celebration necessarily took place after the event, at such short notice that it was quite impossible to notify our families. Phil and Clive had hopes of better things when their own 20th's came along – some months hence – but by that time the situation had changed somewhat, not the least of the changes being that the B.E.F. was no longer in France! I think all 5 of us saw the age of 20 as something of a landmark, if not a watershed, and my own diary tells me that as I passed into a new decade I looked back on one in which so very much had happened, and speculated on what the next ten years would bring – Marriage? A change of job? The fulfilment of my ambitions to go to university? Of one thing I did seem certain – that the next decade would see the end of youth, since at about 25, as I put it, one would surely begin to feel that youth was over! Nearly 50 years on, I permit myself a wry smile.

The Danish/Norwegian upheaval, had we but known it, brought us very near to the end of our time in Dourges. On May 1st the whole of 'Ack' Section set out on a training exercise which took one half of the Section to St. Pol and the other half to Bapaume. Clive and I were together again but this time on our own, manning one of the smaller, 11 Set detachments, based on Bapaume. The weather was fine, the sense of freedom raised our spirits, and we liked what we saw of the little town itself – not least the fact that on our very first night we were free to go to the local cinema and found it to be showing Broadway Melody of 1936 – a film which brought back nostalgic memories of Hall Green's Robin Hood Cinema, where Geoff and I had seen the film soon after it was released.

The days that followed saw us ranging over a wide area around our Bapaume base. It was a powerful, almost oppressive experience to find ourselves, as soldiers in a second European war, manoeuvring over the haunted countryside which less than a quarter of a century earlier had been the scene of the blood bath of the Somme battles; driving through French villages which were still household names in our own country; erecting our aerial on the sites of battles in which our fathers had fought, and which by 1940 had already achieved a grim immortality. The spirit of those not too distant days seemed to brood over the whole countryside of the Somme. Great tracts remained devastated and untouched, and one of them, which had been specially railed off, identified a particular piece of ground on which more men had fallen than on any other area of comparable size. The immense and beautifully tended war cemeteries of the Somme battles we found intensely moving, and perhaps for the first time we began to have some inkling of the reality and meaning of "the lost generation" of which one heard so much in the inter-war years. Further afield at Vimy Ridge, to which our whole Section made a special pilgrimage one day, the Memorial to the 60,000 Canadians who had fallen in that Sector seemed somehow to have captured in stone the whole tragedy of that First World War: I found it awesome and slightly frightening; but above all, sad beyond belief.

During the course of this exercise we saw quite a bit of the French Army and what we saw did not encourage us. Even to our inexperienced eyes much of their equipment seemed poor and out of date, and we could scarcely credit the fact that they still seemed to rely on horses for most of their transport requirements. By our standards, too, the individual soldiers appeared extremely scruffy: daily shaving, for example, was clearly not the norm in the French army; and as for the discipline on the march, even our own Territorial unit seemed like guardsmen by comparison.

The training exercise in which we were engaged turned out to be more than usually interesting, especially one occasion on which we went quite a long way afield, to Hésdin, where we removed our wireless set from its vehicle and carried it up a narrow, winding stone staircase to the top of Hésdin's very high church tower. Our Commanding Officer was there, and we carried out various long-range test transmissions – an activity which seemed far more important and satisfying than that which normally passed for wireless training. On this day too, as on many others, we had passed through magnificent countryside, looking at its best in beautifully sunny spring weather, with trees in bloom for practically every inch of our journey. Returning to Bapaume at the end of the day, I could see, from the back of our wireless truck, the sun setting over the glorious countryside we had passed through earlier in the day, and in my diary I recorded that it was a perfect evening, concluding a most enjoyable day. It was good to have had this experience of France at its best, for two days later, as the Bapaume exercise concluded, "the balloon went up".

Chapter 4

THE DUNKIRK CAMPAIGN: MAY 10-31, 1940

From that final exercise in the country of the Somme we were plunged straight into what must surely rate as one of the most extraordinary campaigns in British military history. On May 10th the Germans invaded Holland and Belgium, which was the signal for our British Expeditionary Force to move immediately to their predetermined position, just east of Brussels. Within less than three weeks the Belgian army, on our left, had surrendered, the French were in complete disarray, the B.E.F. had been squeezed back into a small perimeter around the port of Dunkirk and the beaches to the East of it, and a beginning was being made with the evacuation of the entire British Army.

For me, the campaign lasted three weeks – from May 10 to May 31, and it fell into two parts. For the 5 days from May 10–15th the business of our Signals unit was to provide the communications required for our 48th Division's move into Belgium. 'Ack' Section's wireless vehicles were appropriately deployed along the line of advance and I was one of the two-man crew of a Number 11 set detachment (known to us as 'Bugs'), stationed at a main cross-roads at Orchies. In charge was Slim Ryder, one of the most efficient and likeable of all the reservists and regular soldiers who had been posted to us at the outbreak of war. Slim was a man in his middle twenties and a fine wireless operator, with pre-war active service in Palestine already behind him. Between us, we were responsible for manning the Orchies detachment continuously over the whole of the 5 days period. Once our Division had completed its move, we set off post-haste to join them, near Brussels, where I was immediately moved to one of our larger and more powerful mobile wireless detachments – a Number 9 set, installed in one of the vehicles we called 'Gin-Palaces'. In charge was Corporal Tich Humphreys, a tough, stocky reservist in his mid-thirties, with a gritty North Country sense of humour and something of a reputation as a boxer. He was an absolutely sterling character and an ideal detachment commander. Clive Tonry and I were the two wireless operators, in addition to Tich himself, and an Electrician, Signals, made up the fourth member of our crew.

During the course of this 3 weeks period I maintained in my diary a pretty continuous narrative of all that was happening. The greater part of this was written from the operator's seat in our wireless vehicle, in between messages, often while on the move. With few exceptions it was written up at least daily, and often hour by hour. It is reproduced below exactly as I wrote it at the time, word for word. Re-reading it nearly 50 years later I can be a little embarrassed at times by the rather emotional tone of some of the entries, but it has to be remembered that the young and very inexperienced soldier who kept that diary was scarcely out of his teens: or "Nobbut a boy" as some of our North Country reservists would have put it.

10 May 1940. It's 1.30am on Sunday 12th. I am feeling dead tired and nervy and shall be glad when 2.30 comes, when I think I will wake Slim. Probably due to little sleep and continued air raids. Anyway, here goes to describe Friday's doings:

Woken up by terrific noise of A.A. fire at about 5am, after hearing warning at 3.15. All went outside, and 3 bombers were being fired upon to no effect. When got up (early, as the manoeuvre finishes today and we go back) learned Germany had invaded Belgium & Holland. Made all haste back to Dourges. Scenes of feverish activity there. I'm to go on A2 with Slim Ryder, replacing Boodson, on leave. Off immediately to the border to do traffic control. Highly elated sort of feeling – "Action at last", as it were. Settled at Orchies. In the afternoon had our first taste of real war. Two enemy bombers circled over Orchies, turned, dived, and passed over the field opposite to us, going ever lower and swooped down over the middle of the town, about 200 yards away. We were too excited and ignorant to go for cover till after they had passed, and from a ditch I saw 4 or 5 bombs fall from the first plane onto the middle of the town, falling like eggs, quite visible. The plane following probably dropped its load out of my sight. I felt a most peculiar sensation as I saw the bombs drop – it all seemed unreal and impossible somehow. I felt no actual fear at the time – probably due to ignorance, but a combination of great excitement and horror. The bombs, it transpired, hit the signal box, but without much damage done and no one killed. Loaded rifles in case any more should come as low as that. No fighters and few A.A. after the raiders. At 4.30 [p.m.] the column began to pass. We didn't pass traffic [wireless messages] as were reserve to lines. More raids during course of early evening, and afternoon. Quite accustomed to the noise of A.A., Brens, machine guns, now. As we are on a cross roads, fear they may be after it, as it was the railway – main road junction they were after this morning. Slim tells me Hénin was bombed last night – one woman killed. In evening, as anticipated, a great raid at dusk, over our town and its districts. Bombers came straight over us, and as they passed over our heads the significant whine of bombs began – we had soon learned to recognise it – and we all dived for the ditch, ankle deep and more in horrible green slime, into which my rifle had to fall, barrel first! All of us scared stiff. Bombs fell in the same general direction as at dinnertime and all round us was the thud of bombs and vivid flashes, with tracer and machine gun bullets all over the sky. The heavens seemed full of flying bullets, shells and aeroplanes. They wrecked some houses in the village and killed civilians. Swines! Today was about the biggest thrill – and scare – of my life. Had to work thro' night. Slim woke me about 3 [a.m.] and I had got to bed about 10.30, but D.R.'s [despatch riders] coming in till about 12, with tales of journeys into Belgium, Jerry planes brought down in flames, bombs at Tournai and Brussels, and it was well after 12 o'clock before I got to sleep.

I am going to wake Slim in a minute. I'm dead tired and I can tell from my Morse that my nerves are ragged.

On 11th was on set at 3 in morning. Continual air raid warnings and planes over till quite tired of getting in and out of back of truck to get near ditch with M.P. [Military Policeman] with whom I chatted a lot. This is making me quite nervy, and indeed, everyone else too, as yesterday's efforts were a bit too near home for comfort. No bombs dropped but saw raiders passing over many times. Slim relieved me at 0830, and slept, none too well, till 1100 hrs. No raids during day. Walked into town and saw yesterday's damage. People seem bewildered, and it's really pitiful – as one woman said "We haven't done anything to them. Why are they doing this? Didn't they do enough to us last time?" (The place was in flames last war).

Air raid warnings all day, but no bombs here. Can see them dropping a few miles away.

All over the town, at dusk, the people are on doorsteps, watching for planes. They came but didn't drop here. We are still watching the advance into Belgium.

12 May. Traffic [Wireless messages] as lines have failed. Quite exciting messages passed. One warned M.P.s & D.R.s to watch for a man dressed as officer, in a staff car, going along route of advance into Belgium, burning cable. Another warned of delayed action bombs. Brown, at the other end, is sending and receiving atrociously. Till evening had quite forgotten it is Whit today.

In town saw great hole – large enough to hold a cottage, where bomb had fallen, blown farm outhouses to bits and split farm house in two. Dead calf at bottom of crater. People seem calmer today after temporary respite from bombing. Very tired indeed. Refugees in cars coming through all day long.

13 May. Still at it. Working 24 hours a day between 2 of us. Forgotten again it is Whit Monday. Quite settled down to this routine. As lines are working, are in reserve again, and just maintaining communication.

14 May. Still at Orchies. Lots of air raids. Getting very tired, working these shifts. Believe we may go tomorrow. 48th Div. passing through today but didn't see anyone I knew. In afternoon got a good haircut and – thank goodness – a shampoo.

Was in field with Slim & a lot of youngsters kicking a ball about when 2 bombers dived over town close to us. Ran like hell for rifles and felt rather silly when, with rifles at our shoulder, we noticed the Belgian markings.

15 May. Moved at 1.30. Hell of a quick journey down. When arrived lot of A section there already, and swopped experiences. Felt dead tired and thought I was good for a night's sleep. We and a lot of the Sigs. are in the grounds of a beautiful big house. Hadn't arrived above half an hour when told to go with Tich to gin palace [wireless vehicle with No. 9 set] to work 2 brigades. Means being up all night again, 10,000 curses. Gin palace parked next to small farm, with 2 daughters. Felt quite ill. Fatigue I suppose, and went to bed about 8 o'clock. Tich going on [wireless set] till about 2 or 3 o'clock. Called up at 9.30 however to operate set while Tich went to see C.O., and all C.O. wanted was to know if we were through. Tich very annoyed. Felt much better though already, after rest, and when Tich woke me about 0200 felt quite fresh – in spite of lying awake about 2 hours owing to effects of black coffee. Throughout the evening we could hear a continuous roar of artillery. Was heartbreaking to see the continuous stream of refugees from the direction of the guns.

16th-17th May. On set at 0200. At 6 o'clock saw thrilling air battle. Planes fetched down. Jerries I think. All night, and until 0730, continuous A.A. against planes overhead. Went to bed for a couple of hours 0900. Going to lunch took us nearly all afternoon as it was a long way away. All afternoon and evening continual waves of German bombers going over. Scores of them. Went on set till 2000 and had been in bed about 1½ hours when warned we were moving. Terrific barrage going on round us, and when I got up the farm was full of refugees sleeping all over floor and everywhere – all fled from area around. Germans it appears are attacking, and the glow we can see is Brussels in flames. About 3 miles behind us our artillery is throwing over H.E. Terrific barrage. At 12 o'clock [midnight] up comes Keeling [our Section Officer] very agitated with a D.R. with operation orders. We are to get them out at all costs, OiiU. [Most immediate] In plain language, and orders 144 Bde. to be thrown into support another lot counter-attacking where Germans have broken through. That point is just behind us where we can hear the artillery. Horrible atmospherics and jamming. Get it through however. Keeling in horrible state of suspense walking up and down outside the truck and a tremor in his voice. Must admit I felt very pent up though, especially as I.M.I. [repeat] came back first time. Moved to narrow lane nearby, preparatory to move of Div. H.Q. but hanging around for ages, waiting we thought till 2 or 3 [missing] sets were found. Gunfire getting nearer where Germans have broken through. Sent and received messages, all very important and in clear, and our colonel came into our gin-palace to try to contact 145 Bde. to inform them Divisional Commander on way to see what trouble was all about. Still no move at 0400, and Slim Ryder's set, working artillery, received message indicating Germans only 4 miles away. All except our truck and his move out, and I begin to think we are being left as a decoy to work on and lead Jerry to think Div. is still there. Am told during night that 48 Div. is being thrown in to hold Jerry back and cover retreat to fresh defence line of 1 & 2 Divs. To our relief we left about 0930. Worked on move and arrived about 1200 hrs. (17th) dead beat at a place where we hoped to stay a bit permanently. We were given a wireless silence, but just as we were turning in, we had to start work – very lucky, and I got 4 hours sleep. Extremely busy. Showers of messages. Pips ['immediates'] and all sorts. Orders to move at 1830. I stayed on set as Clive had had next to no sleep, and Tich was driving. Terrible journey – roads crammed with refugees and we went round a long way, to avoid bridges about to be blown up. Working on move all morning, and at 1330 I took off the headphones for the first time since 0200 hrs.

(18th) Absolutely worn out. However no sooner had our trucks arrived at car park than our truck & 3 bugs [wireless vehicles with No. 11 sets] ordered out on a "special mission" with the C.O. We went back forward to the new lines near Ath and worked 144 and 145 brigades who were holding Ath. Absolutely physically and mentally whacked. The electrician fitter of our party has not slept since Tuesday night and it's now Saturday.

We passed some exciting traffic with the brigades. Soon after sending a message that 2 German troop carriers had landed near us, everyone was turned out with rifles as some Germans were "Just down the road". I was on set and felt pretty scared as I daren't leave it as only link with brigades. Must have been beaten off though, or a false alarm. Moved out about 1a.m. with them definitely "on our heels". Closed wireless down and slept in back of gin palace on move. Calculated Clive and I have had 5½ hours sleep in last 77½ hours. Infantry I saw were absolutely played out – fatigued as I have never seen men fatigued. Christ, if this is war I don't know how long any of us will last. General and the brass hats very pleased with our wireless detachment for having maintained communication as we have. I think it surprised everyone. A long weary journey then, through the night with diversions owing to reports of Germans on road ahead of us. Major Jones' [our second in command] car was abandoned at Ath after being hit by machine gun bullets. Woken up about 0500 by sound of machine gun bullets and thought we had run into Germans. Thinking this to be the case I thought this was the tightest spot I had ever been in, but it was alright as it was only an air raid. Our column was being bombed and bombs fell in front and behind us. Eventually we reached an orchard in France, having crossed the border some time earlier.

May 19th Having arrived at the orchard I stripped off, washed well, and slept for a few hours. Numerous air fights, and saw some Jerries brought down, by Spitfires I think. Find farm is empty, and install ourselves. Sleep again in afternoon, and wrote home – a relief as it is ages since I wrote and this is the first day it has been allowed, as up to now, censoring has been impossible. At night all sat round the farm table and drank the beer left in the house and discussed our experiences, which all told were many and varied. MacDonald and Rider had had about the worst up till now, having been forward on the first night of the retreat and were machine gunned, bombed and shelled. Appears our force held out in Belgium, as spearhead, but French and Belgians on our flanks retreated, and to avoid being cut off we had to go back too.

May 20th. Up quite early all things considered – about 0730 and great fun watching the efforts of the B.&.L. [Brutal and Licentious Soldiery] to milk cows. Got lots of tinned food and beer from deserted shop opposite us. Clive said Geoff [who was on leave when the balloon went up] was in a temporary infantry platoon – he had heard from Sid Holland, who had been with him after coming back from leave, but had escaped. Judge my

Clive's impression of the B.&L. complete with life-jacket.

surprise when an hour or two later in walks Geoff. After a long march, and with blistered feet, he had got on a 1 Corps Sigs. lorry after being sent out with other returned from leave men to defend some part of a canal. Too late for the chicken we killed and cooked for lunch, but he was able to join in a fair sized binge we had that night. Very pleasant day all told.

21 May Slept like a log till 0830. Breakfast of eggs, tinned beans, and mushrooms. In morning find we are doing signal duties and guard. I click for permanent guard – not bad though, at 2 hrs 40 mins., compared with 8 hours per day, in the signal office. Boodson and Slim Ryder return. Have had horrible experience. In a wood being shelled by Jerry, up and down, a creeping barrage at about 10 yards intervals. Attached to an infantry company holding the wood and they say when they left, more of the company dead and wounded than alive. It was 8th Warwicks. By a miracle their truck managed always to be between two barrage lines and eventually, theirs being the only transport, they were told to run for it, and report to someone the dreadful position the company were in.

In the afternoon our detachment ordered out to work to some tank outfit. Pleased, as it gets one off the guards. On a farm with 3 beds between 4 of us. Nice work! On set 12 – 4 o'clock. Terrific artillery barrage going on all day, about 5 miles away.

May 22 Went stroll down road with Clive in the morning. Was on set at 4 o'clock, and all afternoon helped Tich prepare etc. a chicken. Tich cooked a fine rice pudding, chicken and chips. Excellent meal! Keeling warns us to be ready to move soon. Moved about 0200 hrs – to fall back on outposts I believe.

All day waves of planes were bombing around us – wonder they missed, because I expect it was us they were after, on strength of D.F. reports.

May 23rd. Arrived Auchy in early morning. Cooked breakfast. Got in an empty farm again, but all area not evacuated – a woman and her daughter on a nearby farm ridiculed the idea of leaving. Geoff gone out again on "special mission". After coming off set in afternoon went to bed and slept until I was woken, about 1900 hours, by terrific bomb explosions. For about 2 hours wave after wave of bombers came over, dropping bombs all round us. Must have dropped at least 100. Not a fighter up against them! In fact since I saw 2 at our first rest about 5 days ago, I have seen none at all. Very little A.A. fire too. On set at 2200 hrs. Dark and lonely in field, and as warning of Jerries around, had my rifle ready with one up the spout.

May 24th. Woke up about 7 and were once more bombed by wave after wave of bombers – bombs landing all around us. During night showers of Warwicks had arrived coming back from the line, and also lots of French cavalry who were going up to relieve us. Many tales from the Warwicks. The 8th practically wiped out – 475 wounded, 275 dead and all except 1 in C Coy. wiped out. Told tales of Jocks who had replaced them (the 7th). They themselves had machine gunned scores of Jerries. Jocks relieved them half drunk, and without orders made a bayonet charge and wiped out 500 Germans. Trying all afternoon to raise station we were working (dangerously) calling every 10 minutes for 3 hours. Find eventually other station ordered at their end not to open up. Moved out about 6 o'clock and went to a place where all our section were congregated. Saw Arthur [Hilliar]. He had had many bad shellings – shrapnel hole in his bus. Geoff's bus in horrible mess – been hit by huge French lorry. No-one hurt. Sleeping in air-raid shelter in middle of hay-rick. Geoff, Clive, Phil and I on guard – hand picked. However our bus and one other 9 set, plus two or 3 11 sets fetched out at 0030 and told we were off to Calais where a German attack was expected at dawn – about 0800 when we arrived at a place near Dunkirk – our apparent destination, and we stopped. Bombed on way down and also on way from Auchy to place we just left.

25th May Hanging around all morning at this place on the outskirts of Dunkirk. Bombed heavily in morning. Wave after wave of bombers absolutely unopposed by fighters – beginning to think our air force has retired. Also 22 Messerschmitts came over. Everyone dead tired after being up all night. No food all day. From what I can see we are surrounded, with us occupying and defending the coast except for Boulogne, which seems to be in German hands, with the Germans in a semi-circle closing in on us. News on wireless seems to think situation very serious. Heavier forces have broken through the gap than was at first thought, and the gap is still open. For the life of me cannot work out our lines and positions. All very complicated. Hear that our line of communication is cut off therefore no post and no rations, and whole of B.E.F. on half rations – which seems to mean nothing at all if today is any criterion. Still I am confident we shall pull through and the only weakness to my mind, are the French and Belgians. Beginning to think British character is, after all distinct from all others. Everyone seems so calm and we have done so well in spite of retreat from Belgium, which I hated and which was due, I believe, to collapse of French and Belgians. All this in spite of our division being criticised by reservists etc. as inefficient. Went to Dunkirk by roundabout route in afternoon to get to new Div. H.Q. Dunkirk heavily bombed – we ourselves bombed on the way to Div. H.Q. Sent out to 144 Bde. Hilliar on D.S. [Directing Station] this time. Moved from there forward up line with 144 Bde. [Wormhout] Arrived in early hours. Stew up!

Didn't know if I needed sleep or food most. Food won, and I wasted 20 minutes sleeping time. Hadn't slept for nearly 48 hours.

May 26th. On set 9–12. Signal officer here not at all keen on wireless. In the last show he was shelled for 6 hours and lost 2 of our K section; when the 9 set was D.F.'d. On this new front, we come under 3 Corps. Very cheerful wireless news put every one in good spirits. War over in a month, etc. Very cheering after dismal news of yesterday. Very matey sort of infantry officer sleeping in an out house with us and his men. Though O.K. to us he treats his men like dirt – though it is probably a superficially "tough" way of talking to them. Magnificent chateau here. We are in a sheltered grove in its grounds. Beautiful target though! When on [wireless] set, wire behind switch fused and little flame shot up. Temporarily repaired. Infantry sergeant here tells us of hell of a time he had in Belgium – shelled to hell, surrounded, etc.

May 27. On set in morning. Important messages passed. German tanks broken through French. 80 Armoured cars about 5 miles away. Everyone in pent up state of preparedness. Devastating dive bombing in afternoon – probably 30 bombs dropped round us, not more than 70–100 yards away, I should think. Nearest to real fear I have ever been, but reasonably calm – cowering under a wall with foundations of building shaking like hell every time a bomb dropped. We would hear a whistle after the roar of the diving engine, and then a shuddering explosion. Infantry officer in our out-house very drunk. Woken up by bombs and must have thought he was going over the top or something such, for he tore round giving hackneyed encouragement to his men and a "pep talk" as Clive described it. At the time everyone was worked up. Great explosions all round – Jerry hammering Gloucesters a mile or two away, and also said to be in a village about 300 yards away. Infantry men at the moment are manning hastily built trenches in the grounds of our chateau. Have that feeling over me again that I seem to get when we are hard pushed – sort of fatalistic attitude, waiting for it to happen, and mind, as far as thoughts go, almost a blank. Will resume when we are out of this spot of trouble. We are not out but I am resuming all the same.

It is 8 o'clock [p.m.] since my last entry (6.30) we have been shelled like hell. Landing all round us and it seems only a matter of time before one gets us. Hope we shall move out at dark. But ... where can we retreat to? Only to the sea. I suppose what we shall do if we do fall back is defend the port of Dunkirk like blazes. They seem to be all round us. What a life!

May 28. [Although we were unaware of it at the time, on this day the notorious Wormhout [Esquelbecq] massacre of 85 unarmed prisoners from our Brigade's Royal Warwickshire Regiment was taking place just down the road from us]. 0900hrs Pressure eased during night but intense as ever now. Bombs, shells, and, worst of all, the rifle and machine gun fire seems to be only a matter of yards away. 1000hrs. Apparently surrounded. 3 tanks just gone up road 25 yards from us – wood in between, so cannot be sure they were Jerries. Asked by infantry sergeant to man trenches just deserted by his men who have gone a bit forward to reinforce the front line – about 100 yards away, I would say, judging from proximity of rifle and machine gun fire. 1100 hrs Tich and I on set. Rest of odd files sent to defend chateau itself, up the drive, as a few hundred Germans and some armoured vehicles have broken through near to us and they must be wiped out. 1230 hrs being shelled like hell. Whistling over in all directions. Must be completely cut off. Trying to get through to Div. on our set.

145 brigade completely cut off. Poor old Ted. [My sister's boy friend] Machine gun fire getting nearer. 2 o'clock. Took to trenches near truck for a bit as rifle bullets spattering the trees which are between us and the road. 3 o'clock News of tanks in village next to us. Village is on other side of the road from the chateau – about 150 yards away. Woe is us! Village is blazing. 4 o'clock (written after) I was lying on my stomach in a field with sights set at 300 yds. There was a ring of us like that, waiting for Jerry to come. He came on the right flank of the ring. I was on the left, about 150 yds away, and the rifle and machine gun fire from both sides was terrific. I honestly never expected for one moment to get away. They quietened down, and withdrew half of us to a Rear Bde. H.Q. I was one of those left to cover the retreat. About 1½ hours after I first lay down we also were withdrawn, having laid all the time in torrential rain with no shelter at all. I was simply saturated. Then a 4 miles walk to the new H.Q., chiefly over soft ankle deep ploughed fields. Picked up by lorries then, and all of us, the whole mixed lot who had lain in the field, Service corps, Sigs., ordnance, artillery, went to battalion H.Q., brigade having withdrawn still further. We walked, and got lifts, to brigade H.Q., arriving about 10 o'clock, [p.m.] and found our truck which had gone with advance party. Clothes saturated, and about ½ inch of water in my boots. Road to Dunkirk streaming with French and English transport, all apparently going to be evacuated. Never dreamed we had so many troops in the area – can't see why we are retreating.

29th–30th May. Dumped most of kit in morning, as told we must destroy truck later. Went a little way out of town to the cover of a hedge. Waiting all the time for a move. Hanging about for ages. Village we left this morning now bombed to hell. Bombers passing over all the time to attack the convoys on the road. Trucks pouring past all day. By about 3 o'clock very few trucks passing. About 6 o'clock, a great shock, for hordes of troops came running back from the front line, the village down the road which we left this morning. French, black and British came pouring past. No-one seemed to know why they were running. Brigadier turns out brigade H.Q. to man the ditches, for apparently something pretty terrible coming up the road. French murmured about Boche and tanks – when they could stop running. We stopped infantry lorry, asked them to give us a Bren gun. Just threw one out to us, without any questions and ammo too. Stopped a C.S.M. [Company Sergeant-Major] who told us how to work it. Infantry man came past on a horse he had mounted – very distressed – had just escaped from a tank – his friend killed at his side.

Once more could not see how we could possibly get out of this spot. Saw a party advancing towards us from the village: just in time found they were remnants of British infantry lot. Again, later, a party with a white flag was spotted. Slim sent to meet them. Found they are French. About 8 o'clock [p.m.] given orders to destroy set and vehicles. Thought this silly as we are 20 miles out from Dunkirk and we might as well ride as far as we can. Couldn't understand it when I was told we are not moving out till midnight as there is nothing at all between us and the enemy down the road. Whole brigade – remnants, that is, started to march at midnight. Ring of burning towns and villages all round us. Star shells and flares going off all round. At midnight started the worst march I have ever done in my life. Single file most of the way as dumped lorries blocked the road. Full kit. Flaming lorries. Absolute exhaustion. Walked for 6 hours with 10 minutes rest each hour and each hour worse than the last. Last 5 or 6 miles through tightly packed French horses dumped by French. Many dead horses and men on the route. Apparently not going to Dunkirk but some sands about 11 km.

East of it. For miles could see the pall of smoke over Dunkirk from that flaming oil. During last 2 hours had no 10 minutes break as when we reached the head of the brigade column, which had got split up a bit, going through French horses, we got with the Warwicks who had already finished their rest. Saw with them a really fine bit of soldiering. All the French and many of the English were just straggling along, a proper rabble, and the colonel of the Warwicks formed up what was left of his men – including us – in threes, gave the word of command, and set off at the head of his column. He was wounded I think, in the leg, for he was limping.

There they were, in step, about 40 of us, someone even playing the mouth organ at the end of what was the most gruelling march they had ever had, after 3 weeks of continuous fighting, no sleep, and fighting a rear guard retreating action all the way. We went the last miles through densely packed horses left by the French, until the road opened out again, and then occurred what I have just described. We thought when we reached the outskirts of a village that we were there, but no, it straggled on for about 3 miles and then we left the Warwicks – an officer said as they passed "Well done Warwicks – thanks very much!" We went to the shores and walked about 2 miles up and down soft sand – agony of agonies after our march – looking for our unit. Huge masses of men, and apparently only way of getting on a boat was to wade. Hung about a bit and eventually got in with some Sigs. and we all formed up as part of a great 3-sided square controlled by our own colonel – a few thousand men all told, I should think. Dead all over the beach. Continual alarms as aircraft pass over. Dead weary and aching all over. Tich went to sleep – too weary to bother about trying for a boat, but when we formed into the square he came with us.

Party of 10 of us detailed to try to get onto a boat – one of the many floating derelict, for it was difficult to board them, and they were sinking or half filling with water and being abandoned. Chief trouble was too many men trying to get on a boat. Well, Clive was with our party and when 3 boats – the first a motor driven one – came up to us we tried for that instead of trying to salve a derelict. Clive started wading, and eventually deciding it was inevitable I should get wet if I were to get away, I followed. About up to the armpits when I got on to the second boat. Clive got on the first. Too many tried to get on our boat. It turned broadside and was hit by the pretty heavy waves and sank. Drenched through. Don't know what happened to Clive. Remember seeing Taffy Roberts [one of our reservists] up to his armpits by our boat and telling him it was hopeless to try to get in as overloaded already. I then waded out to a lifeboat with a marine in it. Too many tried to get on it again. Filled with water, and that sank too, so once more I had the same experience.

Staggered to the shore exhausted and collapsed on the stones. Heavy wet clothes and full kit, less rifle dropped when the first boat turned over, had reduced me to such a state that I didn't care if I did die. Continual wading into a heavy sea had also sapped my strength, and at the end of that 3 weeks .... I decided it was impossible to get a boat and for the third successive day gave myself up as finished. After a time I looked around a bit and saw blokes trying to get out to the destroyer in all sorts of queer craft – light canvas boats, rubber ones – impossible for them to get out really. Then, final blow, the last destroyer went. However, about a quarter of an hour later I saw 3 boats in a string, with blue jackets in them. As a last final effort I started wading. The first 2 wouldn't pick me up as they said go back to the shore, and they would come, but hundreds of men were there all waiting for the boat. The third boat stopped. I went to the far side to stop it overbalancing, as someone else was trying to get in the near side. I simply could not heave myself in and it was with the greatest possible effort that I raised my leg and was dragged in by the fellows already on the boat. As it was absolutely necessary to row, got energy to paddle from some source I never dreamed was there. Started off to cargo boat that was nearby and finished off the journey being towed by a motor boat.

As we arrived at boat, many other boats arrived and delayed our boarding, and all the time had to keep our boat away from the side of the ship with an oar. Really can't imagine how I did it – seemed hours.

Once aboard poured into hold. Saw Harvey and Boodson. Changed after a fashion – luckily my blanket [on top of my pack] had kept water out of pack, and had a spare shirt and pants. Went into a dozing sleep after eating bits of bully beef – all I could remember eating in the last 3 days bar some beans eaten cold. Kept waking up, and at about 6 o'clock [p.m.] sighted England. Went on deck in preparation. Terrifically cold – had put on again my wringing wet trousers – and I lay shivering uncontrollably, dozing till, I think, about 1 o'clock [on 31 May] when we landed at Margate – delay being apparently due to minefields etc. Went to casualty clearing station on bus, and saw best sight in the world – clean clothes, bread and butter, and water for washing. Went straight to train after, and got some food for train. Ate it and went to sleep like a log. Woke up at a London station – cheering crowds etc., and had lots of food brought to us. Travelled onwards, and are apparently not going to Reading as I thought.

Chapter 5

AND AFTERWARDS... 1940

The Dunkirk evacuation generated in Britain an intensity of national emotion the like of which has probably never been known before or since. The sudden realisation that the whole of the B.E.F. was trapped with its back to the sea, with nowhere to retreat to and no realistic alternative to capture by the all-conquering German army; the glimmer of hope as our navy – and the small boats – came in to begin the evacuation of our troops from Dunkirk and its beaches; the gradually mounting scale of their success in getting the troops away; the final realisation – almost too much to dare to believe – that virtually the whole of our British Army in France seemed likely to be saved, and live to fight another day: small wonder that in those few action-packed days the nerves of the whole nation, and above all those whose men-folk were numbered amongst the quarter of a million British soldiers in France – were at full stretch, as day succeeded day, and the successful evacuation continued.

For us – the troops who were evacuated – the anxiety, the relief, the general state of emotion, communicated itself to us the moment we set foot on shore, and likewise at every railway station, full of cheering crowds, that our tightly packed troop trains passed through, as they bore us away from the channel ports where we had landed. For most of us the first priority was to get news of our safe arrival through to our families – not easy to achieve when telephone lines were blocked solid with calls, and letters would not get through until the next day. But the telegraph service worked wonders for many – and costs were often waived for evacuated soldiers with no English money to their names. Civilians at various stations, anxious to help, would take messages written by soldiers on scraps of paper, and pass them on to relatives. Split up by the evacuation, and separated from their friends, soldiers who had arrived in England would nevertheless try to reassure the parents, wives and families of those friends. Geoff Newman, for example, who arrived in England a day before I did, sent a telegram to his mother in which he asked her to tell my mother that I was following shortly: in fact we had not seen one another for days. I myself, in a brief letter to my girl friend despatched on the day of my arrival, said that I thought her brother, Ken Rider, got away around the same time as I did, that I had heard he had got a boat, and that there was no need to worry. In fact he was a full day behind me, and amongst the very last to be evacuated.

Train after train carried the newly arrived and totally disorganised troops to temporary destinations in all parts of the country, from whence the complex process of sorting them out and reassembling them into their parent formations speedily got under way. I myself, with two of 'Ack' Section, one of whom was fellow-librarian Ken Boodson, left Margate where we had landed, for a 14 hour train journey which finally took us to the little mining town of Alfreton in Derbyshire. There we were received with the most wonderful hospitality and kindness on all sides.

Within a few days those of us who belonged to 48 Div. Sigs. found ourselves en route for Hereford, where the widely scattered elements of our parent unit were being reassembled. The excitement of being reunited with friends we had last seen while the retreat was in full progress knew no bounds, but in the forefront of our minds was a deep anxiety. By this time we were aware that the entire 145 Brigade of our 48th Division, including many 'Ack' Section members, had been lost at Cassel. As it became clear to the wives and parents of these men that they were not amongst the fortunate majority who had safely returned to England, sad little notices began to appear in the Birmingham Mail, asking for information from survivors about husbands and sons who had been reported missing. Eventually it came to be known that most of 145 Brigade had in fact been taken prisoner, but many anxious weeks were to drag by before their families received notification of this; and there were those, of course, for whom the notification was of husband or son being killed in action or having died from wounds. The several members of 'Ack' Section who became P.O.W.'s included Phil Vane, one of our group of five school friends; Arthur Hillier, the reservist who had been my detachment commander during the Danish/Norwegian 'flap'; Bill Cody, and several other good friends. Close to home, too, was the capture of Ted Lane, my younger sister's boy friend, who belonged to the Section of our Signals unit that was permanently attached to the 145th Brigade. Though many Birmingham and Midland homes had reason to rejoice at the "Miracle of Dunkirk", there were others for whom the defeat of the B.E.F. in France marked the beginning of five years of anxiety and misery.

The ultimate destination of the re-constituted 48th Division was the Southwest of England, where it was to be responsible for home defence, and our 'Ack' Section soon found itself in Devonshire, where it was brought up to strength and, slowly, re-equipped. For many months during that anxious summer of 1940, 'parashot' duties – looking out for and guarding against German airborne landings – took priority over signals duties (though had paratroops in fact descended, what we should have resisted them with could have been known only to the good Lord!) In due course, however, 'Ack' Section's wireless detachments, re-equipped and up to strength, were deployed over the whole of Devonshire and parts of Somerset and Cornwall, providing the wireless communications for the newly emergent 48th Division. To complete the story of the 48th Div. Sigs., its Headquarters and No. 1 Company (which included 'Ack' Section) became in due course the back-bone of the 78th Divisional Signals. The 78th was a famous division which served with very great distinction in the North African Campaign of 1942 and the Sicilian and Italian campaigns, from 1943 until the end of the war.

In three tumultuous weeks the campaign which led to the evacuation of the B.E.F. from Dunkirk and its beaches had transformed the raw Territorials of the 48th Div. Sigs. into "old soldiers". We had experienced enough at the hands of the Germans to know that we were in for a long war and a difficult one. We believed – rightly – that we had been badly let down by the French and the Belgian armies, and most of us were unaware at that time of the contributory shortcomings of the top leadership of the B.E.F. itself. Our ignominious ejection from France had therefore provided at the most only a tiny dent to our confidence. We in the returned B.E.F. were told by the nation's leaders – both civilian and military – that we were the seasoned nucleus from which would be built the army that would finally defeat Hitler. We believed it, and the attitudes of most of us changed accordingly. Our group of school friends, now reduced to four, though continuing to adopt a pretty light-hearted attitude towards life, were no longer the irresponsible thorn in the flesh of those in authority that they had been in those pre-Dunkirk days; indeed, they began to see themselves as N.C.O.s or even officers in the new armies that were starting to be built. Their careers during the rest of the war could certainly not have been predicted from the history of their first 9 months in the army, when they had been little more than sky-larking schoolboys, and neither could the careers of my three fellow librarians – as the following brief account of their army service up to demobilisation will show.

Pride of place should probably go to Clive Tonry, who left 48 Div. Sigs. in 1941 for the Guards Armoured Division, as a corporal. From thence to O.C.T.U. in 1943, and in 1944, as a second-lieutenant with 159 Lorried Infantry Brigade, he took part in the Normandy landings and was awarded the Croix de Guerre with Silver Star for gallantry in the battle of Odon Bridgehead. Of his distinguished post-war military career, more shortly.

Of my three librarian colleagues, Ken Boodson, who was brilliant in technical matters, went on to achieve Warrant Officer status as a Foreman of Signals, and to serve in West Africa. Harry Sargeant's abilities earned him very rapid promotion after his return from Dunkirk. By mid-1941 he was a full sergeant and soon afterwards he was posted to 42nd Armoured Division, and subsequently to 79th Armoured Division. He was with that Division during the Normandy landings, was mentioned in despatches, went on to take part in the Rhine crossings, and was demobilised in September 1945. Ken Rider remained with 'Ack' Section when it became part of the 78th Divisional Signals, and was with that Division throughout its memorable progress from the 1942 North African landings with the First Army, on to the 1943 invasion of Sicily and Italy, with the Eighth Army, and then the gruelling Italian campaign, including the attack on Cassino – a campaign which continued until V.E. Day in May 1945. By the time he was demobilised he had the satisfaction of finding himself a senior N.C.O. in the 'Ack' Section which he had joined at the outbreak of war.

Of the rest of our group of school friends, Maurice Brett, who even before the war was something of a wireless expert, became a staff sergeant, and Geoff Newman and I, as lance-corporals, went off together to O.C.T.U. in August 1941. We were separated after being commissioned in 1942, and Geoff spent virtually all the rest of the war as Signals Officer to the 3rd Medium Regiment, Royal Artillery. He served with them in Egypt, Palestine, Syria, Italy, France, Belgium and Germany, and was mentioned in despatches. He was demobilised with the rank of Captain. I myself was posted to 11 L. of C. Signals soon after being commissioned, and with that unit took part in the landings in North Africa in 1942 and the landings on the Italian mainland in 1943. I stayed with that unit until well after the end of hostilities, becoming Captain and Adjutant for a short period, and finally serving for a few months as Staff Captain(Q) at G.H.Q., Central Mediterranean Forces, before demobilisation in May 1946.

On demobilisation the primary concern of all ex-servicemen, after an absence of anything up to 6 or 7 years with His Majesty's forces, was to re-establish themselves in civilian life as quickly as possible. In many cases this led to moves away from pre-war bases and home-towns, and this was certainly true of the group of 5 school friends and the 4 Birmingham librarians who have been the central characters in my story. As the years passed we had, with few exceptions, lost contact with one another, but in 1979, the 40th Anniversary of the outbreak of war, I made a determined effort to get in touch with each and every one of them, and to arrange a re-union dinner in Birmingham. My enquiries yielded the sad information that Maurice Brett had died five years previously, but all the others were located, and with the exception of Geoff Newman, who was in South Africa, all were present at the Birmingham reunion in September 1979, plus one other – Ted Lane, the boy friend of my younger sister, who had become her husband on demobilisation; he had been captured at Cassel with our 145 Infantry Brigade.

This 40th Anniversary reunion was a happy occasion, full of nostalgia and reminiscence, and we decided to meet thereafter annually, in locations which had some special significance for members of 'Ack' Section of the 48th Divisional Signals. On two of these occasions Geoff Newman, over from South Africa, was able to join us, and our reunion group has twice found itself in the Chilton Foliat/Hungerford area (where the Fowl Pen stands unchanged except that its roof is no longer of thatch), in Hereford, in Bradford-on-Avon, in Devonshire and, in recent years, back in Birmingham. The high-light has been a 5 day visit to France and Belgium, which four of us were able to make in 1984, in the course of which we re-traced the whole of our Division's progress during those momentous days of May,1940. Inevitably, as we all moved through our 60's, and in some cases into the early 70's, death has taken its toll of our group, and Ted Lane, Harry Sargeant and Ken Boodson are very sadly no longer with us.

Not surprisingly, much of our talk at the reunions has been of those early days of the war, up to and including Dunkirk. What is clear is that after nearly 50 years, the memory of those first nine months with 'Ack' Section of the 48th Div. Sigs. has stayed with us more permanently, more indelibly, than any of the many and very varied experiences which were to come our way in the several years of war which were to follow Dunkirk. It is also a fact that I am by no means the only member of our reunion group who believes that after the sudden shock of the 3 weeks campaign which led to Dunkirk – and particularly that first nightmare experience of being dive-bombed, and the ultimate evacuation from the beaches – nothing which was to follow could hold many terrors for us. It is also the general view that having come safely through those war-time years, we found that our army experience has undoubtedly given an extra and beneficial dimension to our post-war lives and to the careers which we have followed. Those careers have been both interesting and varied, and it is perhaps not inappropriate to conclude this small book with a brief outline of how our group of five school friends and my 3 fellow librarians have lived out their post war years.

Ken Rider, after returning to Birmingham Reference Library, rose to be Head of that library's specialised Science and Technology Section. In 1972 he was appointed first Librarian of Birmingham's newly founded Polytechnic and saw it successfully through the complexities and challenges of its early years, before retiring in 1977. After retirement he joined Birmingham University's Shakespeare Institute where he carried out research and completed a thesis on Shakespeare's Portrayal of Old Age, a unique study for which he was awarded the degree of Master of Arts. In recent years he has given much of his spare time to writing verse, including a long poem entitled The Road to Dunkirk, and another, on the Falklands war, which will be published shortly (died 2001).

Clive Tonry remained in the regular army after the end of the war, and following 3 years in Airborne Signals went to Staff College. By 1953 he was a Lieutenant-Colonel and Military and Naval Attaché in Rangoon, Burma. After experience at the Ministry of Defence, a variety of regimental duties in Britain, and a command of his own – the 8th Signals Regiment – he was awarded the O.B.E., and moved on, as a full Colonel, to a range of postings which included that of Defence, Military and Air Attaché at the British Embassy in Bulgaria, Commander Royal Signals in Singapore, and Colonel General Staff at the Ministry of Defence's Signals Directorate. From 1971 to 1972, when he retired, he was a Brigadier General Staff at the Ministry of Defence and Deputy Signal Officer in Chief. Scarcely, perhaps, the career that would have been predicted in 1940 for the composer of the famous protest poster about excessive fatigues! (see page 53). Since retirement from the army Brigadier Tonry has enjoyed a happy and successful career as teacher and Bursar at a boys' preparatory school.

The troopship which took Geoff Newman to join the Eighth Army in Egypt had halted a while at Cape Town – long enough for Geoff to meet and fall in love with the lady who was to become his wife when he returned there, shortly after demobilisation. The trainee accountant of 1939 joined one of South Africa's largest finance houses – Syfrets Trust

– and rose to become one of its Directors. Now retired, he has discovered a latent talent as an artist, and his paintings are of sufficient quality to qualify for inclusion in important exhibitions (died 2001).

Ken Boodson's career after demobilisation was spent with I.C.I. Metals, which was later to become I.M.I. As Chief Group Librarian and Information Officer he re-shaped that vital aspect of I.M.I.'s activities, and became a leading national figure in the field of industrial library and information work. Ken took early retirement in 1974, for health reasons, and was an enthusiastic attender at our reunions until his death in 1987.

Phil Vane, who had been captured at Cassel, spent the next 5 years in Prisoner of War camps. He attempted, unsuccessfully, to escape, and the very heavy labour to which he was subjected included work in a stone quarry, and underground in coal mines. On demobilisation he returned to the Building Surveyor's Department of the Birmingham Corporation, becoming an Assistant Building Surveyor before moving to Liverpool as a Divisional Building Surveyor. There followed several years in which he ran the family business and a period with building industry products manufacturers before he moved some 20 years ago to his present work as a life insurance and pensions specialist. Soon after the end of the war Phil rejoined the Territorial Army as a signalman, was commissioned in 1950 as a full lieutenant, and achieved the rank of major before leaving the T.A. in 1960. He had the very special satisfaction of commanding a squadron of the unit in which he had served with the B.E.F. in 1940 – the 48th Divisional signals!

Ted Lane, like Phil, had been captured at Cassel, and had spent five grim years in P.O.W. camps. On demobilisation he trained as a teacher and became one of Birmingham's best known and most highly regarded primary school headmasters. There can be little doubt that his time as a P.O.W., which included work underground in the mines of Silesia, was a contributory factor to his untimely death in 1985, just a few weeks before he was due to retire.

Maurice Brett, as I have mentioned, had died some 5 years before 1979, when our reunions commenced. Thus was cut short what would clearly have been a highly successful career in Birmingham Corporation's

BBC 2004 promotion for Dunkirk Docudrama (Courtesy of The Daily Telegraph).

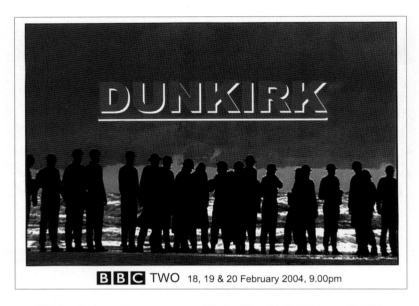

BBC TWO 18, 19 & 20 February 2004, 9.00pm

BBC advance Programme publicity 'Dunkirk' February 2004.

You are invited to attend the Cast and Crew screening of

DUNKIRK

Sunday 15 February 2004 at 10.30am

BAFTA
195 Piccadilly
London W1J 9LN

RSVP
Juliet Dennis
BBC White City Building
Room 5426
201 Wood Lane
London W12 7TS
T: 020 8752 52507
Email: juliet.dennis@bbc.co.uk

Invitation for Wilf Saunders to 2004 BBC 'Dunkirk' Preview.

At BBC 'Dunkirk' Preview 2004.

Wilf Saunders with actor Michael Legge, 2004. BBC 'Dunkirk'.

1st Feb '05

Dear Mr Saunders,

Firstly let me apologise for replying to your very kind letter so late; I have been working abroad and only received it quite recently. I really appreciated the time you took to put pen to paper + your compliments about my performance in 'Dunkirk'. It was such an honour to meet you + your family + I am delighted that you think we did your story proud + just. Though incredibly nervous about meeting you, I was very excited to and (thankfully) my nerves were quashed with

how personable + friendly you were.

It is indeed difficult to play a 'real' person and the pressure to perfect the character can be a struggle, but within the part I found a great strength of character + a genuine humanity in 'Wilf' which helped me hugely. You experienced such horrors and brutality that no man should — for that and for all that you have accomplished to this date, I respect you greatly. God willing, perhaps our paths will cross again soon

Yours Sincerely

Michael Legge

Letter of thanks to Wilf Saunders from Michael Legge, Feb 1st, 2005.

British Broadcasting Corporation Television Centre Wood Lane London W12 7RJ Telephone 020 8743 8000

Professor Wilf Saunders

30th January 2004

Dear Professor Saunders,

Dunkirk

As you may already know, after over two years in development and production, we now know the transmission date for *Dunkirk*. The series will transmit on BBC TWO on 18th, 19th and 20th February at 9.00pm. In addition, there will be an interactive service available to digital viewers, featuring interviews with Dunkirk veterans (please find further details attached).

I know that Lisa has already visited you recently to show you *Dunkirk*, but we are holding a Cast and Crew screening at BAFTA prior to transmission and, as someone who has helped enormously with the development of *Dunkirk*, we would very much like to invite you to attend. The screening will take place on Sunday, 15th February 04. Your invitation is enclosed and I look forward to meeting you in person should you be able to be present (see invitation for RSVP details).

Finally, I would like to take this opportunity to thank you very much on behalf of the whole team including Alex Holmes, Lisa Osborne, Neil McKay, Wanda Koscia and Sarah Barton, for your help during our research – we really couldn't have done it without you!

With very best wishes

Rob Warr
Producer, Dunkirk

Letter of thanks from BBC to Wilf Saunders January 30th 2004.

Wilf Saunders wearing Medals & CBE, Remembrance Day 1995.

Campaign Stars, Clasps and Medals

instituted in recognition of service
in the war of 1939-45

NUMBER OF STARS, MEDALS, CLASPS or EMBLEMS ENCLOSED

Order of Wearing	Description of Ribbon	Clasp or Emblem (if awarded)
1 1939-45 Star	Dark blue, red and light blue in three equal vertical stripes. This ribbon is worn with the dark blue stripe furthest from the left shoulder.	Battle of Britain
2 Atlantic Star	Blue, white and sea green shaded and watered. This ribbon is worn with the blue edge furthest from the left shoulder.	Air Crew Europe or France and Germany
3 Air Crew Europe Star	Light blue with black edges and in addition a narrow yellow stripe on either side.	Atlantic or France and Germany
4 Africa Star	Pale buff, with a central vertical red stripe and two narrower stripes, one dark blue, and the other light blue. This ribbon is worn with the dark blue stripe furthest from the left shoulder.	8th Army or 1st Army or North Africa 1942-43
5 Pacific Star	Dark green with red edges, a central yellow stripe, and two narrow stripes, one dark blue and the other light blue. This ribbon is worn with the dark blue stripe furthest from the left shoulder.	Burma
6 Burma Star	Dark blue with a central red stripe and in addition two orange stripes.	Pacific
7 Italy Star	Five vertical stripes of equal width, one in red at either edge and one in green at the centre, the two intervening stripes being in white.	
8 France and Germany Star	Five vertical stripes of equal width, one in blue at either edge and one in red at the centre, the two intervening stripes being in white.	Atlantic
9 Defence Medal	Flame coloured with green edges, upon each of which is a narrow black stripe.	Silver laurel leaves (King's Commendation for brave conduct. Civil)
10 War Medal 1939-45	A narrow central red stripe with a narrow white stripe on either side. A broad red stripe at either edge, and two intervening stripes in blue.	Oak leaf

List of WW2 Campaign medals, some awarded to Wilf Saunders.

The Under-Secretary of State for War presents his compliments and by Command of the Army Council has the honour to transmit the enclosed Awards granted for service during the war of

1939-45.

Letter sent by Government with Medals.

Parks Department, for Maurice had risen very rapidly after his return from the army, and at the time of his death was holding a very senior managerial post. I understand that to the last he remained a most enthusiastic radio amateur.

Harry Sargeant returned to Birmingham Reference Library after demobilisation, but in 1947 he was appointed to be Worcestershire's first County Archivist, a post which he held with great distinction until his retirement in 1974. During that period he became a leading figure in the British archive world, and served as Chairman of the Society of Archivists. The pioneering and innovative County Record Office which he created at Worcester came to be generally regarded as a model of its kind. Within Worcester itself Harry was a well-known and well-loved public figure, and his many local activities included Chairmanships of Rotary, Probus and the Archaeological Society. The fine collection of World War II scrapbooks which he compiled – on which I myself have drawn freely in this volume – is an enduring legacy for the historians of the future (died 1986).

The author of this book, Wilf Saunders, was awarded a Further Education and Training Grant after demobilisation; this took him to the University of Cambridge, where he read Economics. After graduation he returned to library and information work and progressed, via a variety of posts, to become in 1963 the founding Director of the University of Sheffield's Postgraduate School of Librarianship, and, in 1968, Professor of Librarianship and Information Science. In 1980 he was President of the Library Association, and from 1981-84 he was first Chairman of the Library and Information Services Council, the body which advises the government on library and information matters. He was awarded the CBE in 1982, and in July 1989 Sheffield University conferred on him the honorary degree of Litt.D. He has been very active internationally, and since retiring from his Chair in 1982, advisory and consultancy work has taken him to all 5 continents. Although he has published extensively on professional matters this present book is his only non-professional publication to date – a labour of love which he has been saving up for the 50th Anniversary of the outbreak of World War II and the Dunkirk evacuation (died 2007).

Appendix I

HARRY SARGEANT'S DUNKIRK CAMPAIGN

Chapter 4 comprises my own highly personal account of the Dunkirk Campaign, exactly as recorded in my diary. Some months after his return from Dunkirk my fellow librarian, the late Harry Sargeant, wrote an account of his own experiences during the three weeks in question. This makes an interesting comparison with my own, and though not in diary form would seem to be based on notes which he wrote while the campaign was in progress. Being written after he had had time to think his way through the chaos of those eventful 3 weeks, Harry's account is more systematic and intelligible than my own diary entries, and it seems to me that our two accounts of the campaign complement one another in an interesting and useful way. With the permission of his widow, Mary, Harry Sargeant's account is set out below:

We were due to return to our billets at Dourges on Friday 10th May. On the way back a woman came out of a house in tears and told us that the Germans had invaded Holland and Belgium. The new aerodrome we had just left was bombed a few hours later and eight men of the A.M.P.C. were killed by machine gunning. When we arrived at Hénin Liétard we just had time to fill up with petrol before proceeding to our respective units – luckily all our kit was on board the trucks. I never saw our billets at Dourges again.

I was at Rear Div. H.Q., working back to 1 Corps H.Q. for a few days, and we stayed at Hénin Liétard, sleeping in a tent on some waste ground adjoining a side street. Air-raids were frequent, but only a few bombs were dropped, causing civilian casualties. On May 12th the 48th Division moved to Bernicourt Chateau near a small place called Roust Warendin. The 1st and 2nd Divisions had already gone to Belgium, and the 48th was the reserve division of the 1st Army Corps. Again we used our tent and all was quiet for a day or two. Bernicourt was a lovely place and nightingales were singing all night in the grounds. On the 14th we moved by night across the Belgian frontier and up through Tournai, Ath and Hal, to Linkebeck, not far from Brussels. I did all the driving on my truck, as the three men I had with me were not very experienced – one couldn't drive at all. We drove usually at night and without lights. Refugees were pouring along the roads from Brussels as we went forward, and we saw German planes bombing towns in the distance. No attack was made on our convoy – we were very fortunate in this respect.

We stayed at Linkebeck for two days only – the gunfire got closer and closer and on the second night we moved back about twelve miles. We found out later that the Germans were within four miles of us and the wireless saved the situation. Throughout the subsequent action the only communications possible were in most cases, dispatch rider and wireless. Moves were made so quickly that there was often no time to lay lines.

From this time onwards it was just a succession of retreats at night – 40 miles in one case – and very unsuccessful attempts to get rest and food during the day. We were bombed continually, especially at dawn, by waves of planes, sometimes 50 at a time. Camouflage was essential and we became very practised at it. We stayed at numerous places whose names I never knew, but eventually we found ourselves back in France at a small place just behind the frontier, Monihin, near St Arnand by 19th May. By this time all the civilian population had become refugees, blocking the roads, everywhere streams and streams of them, going in all directions. My detachment stayed for a day or two in a large farmhouse which had been hurriedly abandoned; the owners had left a meal half eaten, and all the farm animals were wandering about, the cows being very distressed. Some French soldiers milked the cows for us later and we lived in style for a short time. I brought a barometer from there as a souvenir. We were bombed regularly, but no damage was done near us. A piece of A.A. shell came through the roof one day, that was all.

Up till this time my detachment had been with Div. H.Q. or Rear Div. H.Q., but from Mouchin I was sent to Lesdain, on 20 May, where was the headquarters of the 145th Infantry Brigade. From here we worked back to Div. H.Q. and came under the orders of the L Section officer, Lieut. Danielson and his sergeant Greenhalgh. Here I came under shell fire for the first time. I was actually sent out to replace another of Ack Section's trucks which had been hit by a shell, wounding one man and making the truck unusable, but not damaging the wireless set. We were much nearer the front, if there ever was such a thing as a front, but conditions were much "hotter". I learnt to distinguish our shells from those of the enemy and to dive for cover when the latter arrived.

Again it was a question of retreat, as the right flank held by the French had apparently given way and there was a constant threat of our being surrounded. The infantry suffered pretty badly; we had the 4th Ox and Bucks, the 2nd Gloucesters and the 1st Bucks. After retiring as far as Landas by about 23rd May, the 145 Bde. was relieved by the French and I went back to Div. H.Q., which by this time was at Aubers, where the battle of Aubers Ridge was fought in the last war. The 145 Brigade fondly imagined that they were going into a G.H.Q. Rest area on 24 May, but they were soon disillusioned, as they were sent right across the 'horseshoe' now occupied by the B.E.F., to Cassel on the Lille-Dunkirk road, where they had orders to fight to the last. I and my crew, Dunlop, Pearce and Murphy, were sent from Aubers to Cassel to rejoin the Brigade. We went via Sechin and Armentiéres, and everywhere was ruin and desolation, with refugees trudging in all directions. The Germans seemed to be in all places at once. I arrived in Cassel before the Brigade, which came later on during the morning of Sunday 26th May. All was fairly quiet then; Cassel had been bombed and was pretty well wrecked, but no serious air-raids were experienced by us then. The B.E.F. was put on half-rations, very little food was obtainable, but the troops raided the shops and houses and helped out their rations. We had no bread at all. Sleep was a rarity at any time, and we were lucky if we managed to wash, let alone shave.

The truck was stationed in the grounds of a large house at the junction of the roads leading to Lille and Steenvoorde. The infantry were, I think, east and south of Cassel, one battalion being at Hazebrouck. Cassel is very similar to Bridgnorth, being perched on a hill. We were on the S.E. slope of the hill. On Monday the Germans got nearer and gave us hell all day with shells. We had guns pointing in all directions, which was most disconcerting at the time. Adjoining my truck was an anti-tank gun pointing down the road, a battery of field guns and an anti-aircraft gun. The din was terrific and all the windows of the house fell out. The truck was hit by bits of shell in several places, but nowhere vital, and nobody was hurt, luckily. We dug a hole near the lorry and extended various pieces of apparatus so we could work from there. German planes came over in droves, with very little opposition – only a bit of very ineffective A.A. fire. During the whole of the time I was in France I saw no more than 20 British planes – the Germans came over 50 at a time. Fortunately no bombs were dropped too near us.

In the early afternoon [of Sunday 26 May] Sergeant Greenhalgh told us that all of us who were not actually working on the sets (there were now three A Section sets at Cassel, another one had come because of trouble with my set, and the other was attached to a field Regiment of Artillery) had to get their rifles and help the infantry defend Brigade H.Q. as the enemy was almost on us. My two spare men, Pearce and Murphy, and myself went to help cover the approach to the main road from the Lille side. Bren guns were firing above our heads and also in the opposite direction from the top of the ridge. The Germans shelled the road junction continually and ultimately one or more shells burst in the garden where we were, and a piece of shell hit Pearce in the arm, just above the elbow, as he crouched at my side. His rifle was smashed as he held it, a fact which probably prevented worse injury. It was pretty bad as it was; he kept fainting as I bound it up with his first aid dressing, aided by another chap from Brigade H.Q., one of the men in L Section. This chap had a truck handy, and with the help of Murphy, who had rolled down the slope when the shell burst, we carried Pearce into it and the L Section fellow took him to Bde. H.Q. where I heard that he was made fairly comfortable. This left me with two men, Dunlop on the set and Murphy with me. We got into a shallow trench with some infantry, Ordnance Corps and one R.A. anti-tank fellow, and a few Signals people, and waited with rifles and grenades for the Germans to appear. Nothing happened, however, and the firing died down after a time and we went back to Bde. H.Q. where we were told that the enemy had been beaten off.

The shell fire had wrecked the place pretty well and had broken the telephone line between my set and Bde. H.Q. in several places. There was a dead man without head or legs lying at the road junction for hours; I saw various horrors at intervals and could elaborate many isolated incidents. Of course we had no idea of the general situation at all. All we knew was that the Germans seemed to be everywhere, and that reinforcements were being continually asked for and there weren't any free to send to us.

It was decided to move the Bde. H.Q. after dark to a safer spot to the NW of the town, right on the other side. To do this we had to go, not by the direct main road, as it was covered by the enemy, but by a maze of lanes, risking one corner which was said to be covered by enemy fire. It was a terrific dash but no guns opened up on us. During this move, I lost sight of the truck in front, the other wireless lorry which had come to help us out, and got completely lost. We spent an uncomfortable time trying to find out which way to go, including studying the stars. Machine gun tracers were flying across the roads and Verey lights kept on flaring up in the air. A convoy of lorries passed us as we were slowly approaching a main road. We stopped and kept quiet as they looked very much like German. When they had gone we went on again and ultimately encountered a British sentry. He took me to his officer who was in the R.A. This officer said that he himself wasn't sure of his position, but that we could stay with his men if we liked. However, we decided to try and find the 145 Bde. or, failing that, Div. H.Q., so we went on again. A French motor cyclist said we couldn't get to Cassel as it was already cut off, and later some French officers in a car came up and offered to lead us in the direction of Div. H.Q. by a road which they knew to be safe. I followed their car until we encountered another British sentry, who told me that he belonged to the 46th Divisional Signals, so I jumped at the opportunity and sent the French car away. We parked the truck with those of the 46th Div. Sigs. and then fell asleep on the ground. It rained heavily later; Dunlop and Murphy never stirred, but I woke up and crawled under the truck. In the morning I endeavoured to find out whether we could get back to the 145 Bde., but the 46th Signals officer said that all the Divisions were abandoning their stores and trucks and retreating to the coast, the various infantry brigades covering the retreat, and advised us to stay with his unit. We didn't like the idea as we thought we ought to try and get back, so the officer sent me to ask a G staff officer for instructions. This officer told me to stay with the 46th and do whatever they did. We were told that all unnecessary transport and stores were to be dumped and we were to get as much rest as we could during the day as we were to march to the coast when it got dark. We threw most of our kit away, changed into clean clothes if we had any and packed as much food as we could. Things must have got worse, as in the end we loaded as many men on as few trucks as possible and headed hell for leather towards Dunkirk, coming under shell fire once and being bombed continually. We became very adept at diving into ditches by long practice. About ten miles from Dunkirk we dumped the lorries and marched in single files of ten men and one N.C.O. at the side of the road. Naturally we were all pretty well done in, but the 46th Signals were a fine crowd, mainly Scots, and they even managed to whistle and sing as we marched, to the amazement of the French troops and refugees who were all over the place. The 46th Division had been sent to France without any Signals at all, and this crowd was a line party borrowed from G.H.Q. Signals. We couldn't go directly to Dunkirk as it was cut off by the Germans, but stayed the night about six miles or so further up the coast. It poured with rain all night, but we three were lucky enough to find places in a tent pillaged from one of the hundreds of dumped and wrecked lorries which were about. We pitched this tent a few yards from a large bomb crater in a field. We got a bit of sleep and at 6am we marched along the beach to Dunkirk, which was a blazing ruin. A heavy smoke pall lay over the town from burning oil tanks and this saved a lot of lives as there were thousands of troops, British and French, packed in a tight mass on the beach, and a machine gunning plane could have caused havoc. No bombs were dropped while we were there, from 8am till midday on Wednesday 29th May. We moved slowly, nearer and nearer to the stone jetty, shepherded in twos by ratings. We lost Murphy here and nobody has heard of him since. When we were a few hundred yards from the boat a rocket went up and the French ran for their lives; we took no notice, but it must have been a signal because a second or two afterwards a shell burst on the spot, followed by many others. We lay flat until the salvo was over; a man had the back of his head blown off just in front of me and the stone jetty was splattered with blood. One shell landed right on the jetty, but boards were placed over the gap, and we made a dash for the boat which was speedily filled up – it was a fair-sized French steamer – and then we promptly went to sleep. I woke up to find us not far from Dover, but we were unable to put in there and ultimately landed at Folkestone about 6p.m. Here we were put in a train and buckets of water, mugs, chocolate, apples and cigarettes were given to us. I scribbled a postcard to Mary and asked a porter to post it for me – I had only Belgian and French francs with me. In my compartment was a Northumberland fusilier who fell dead asleep and wouldn't wake for hours, not even when some tea was brought to us, and a fellow in the Dorsets who was wearing women's underclothes and had sacking round his feet – he was using a pick-helve for a crutch.

We slept through the night and ended up at Yeovil on Thursday morning at 8 o'clock. We were put on army lorries and taken to an R.A. training camp. Here we had a bath, medical inspection and a change of underclothes, and a good breakfast, the first bread we'd had for over three weeks, and then went to sleep again. Later in the day I rang up Mary and asked her to come down and stay. I fixed up a place for her and she arrived the next day. You can imagine how pleased we were to see each other again. They wouldn't let me have a sleeping-out pass from the 'camp', so I slept out without one and nobody noticed. We had a wonderful time at Yeovil – the only ill effects of France on me were badly blistered feet which took some time to heal.

Appendix II

GLOSSARY OF TERMS USED
IN THE DUNKIRK DIARY

A.A.	Anti-Aircraft (guns and search lights) Also known as Ack Ack
A.A.	Automobile Association
A.F.S.	Auxiliary Fire Service
A.M.P.C.	Auxiliary Military Pioneer Corps
A.R.P.	Air Raid Precautions
A.T.S.	Auxiliary Territorial Service
Balloon Went Up	Proper start to WW2 (see Phoney War)
Bde.	Brigade
Billet	Living Quarters for Soldiers
B.E.F.	British Expeditionary Force
B.P.L.	Birmingham Public Library
Croix De Guerre	French Military Bravery Award for act of heroism
Crown & anchor	Dice Game with Mat for Betting
Demobilisation	Official Discharge of person from the Forces
D.F.	Direction finding
D.R.	Despatch rider
Div. (or Divn.)	Division of Troops
Fait Froid	Turned out cold
Fatigue	Army Duty
G.H.Q.	General Headquarters
Gin Palace	Lorry used by Signals as mobile Radio Base
Gun Limber	Field Gun – the wooden cart or 'undercarriage'

H.E.	High Explosive
Housey housey	Old name for Bingo
H.Q.	Headquarters
I.C. (engine)	Internal combustion (type of engine)
i/c	In charge
Jankers	Punishment for minor breach of Discipline
Jingoism	Extreme Nationalism
L. of C. Signals	Line of Communications Signals
L.D.V.	Local Defence Volunteers (Home Guard)
N.C.O.	Non Commissioned Officer
M.P.	Military Police
O.C.T.U.	Officer Cadet Training Unit
Old Sweats	Experienced soldiers
Pals Battalion	Locally raised section of troops. e.g. from same town, university etc.
Phoney War	First few months after War was declared when everyone alert, but no major action for our troops
P.B.I.	Poor bloody Infantry
P.O.W.	Prisoner of War
P.S.I.	Permanent Staff Instructor
R.A.	Royal Artillery
Recce.	Reconnoitre. Gain information in advance.
Red Tabs	Staff Officers
Reservists	Older troops who left Armed Forces before start of War, but held 'on reserve' and then called up to fight
R.S.M.	Regimental Sergeant Major
Sigs.	Signals
T.A.	Territorial Army – see Territorials
Territorials	Volunteer Reserve Soldiers
W.A.A.F.	Womens Auxiliary Air Force

Appendix III

B.B.C. DOCUDRAMA DUNKIRK (2004)

Transcription of WLS handwritten notes

On receiving from Margaret Barnett a nearly full page spread in the Birmingham Post headed in very large type DUNKIRK DIARY: *How the words of a Birmingham teenager helped inspire a major three part B.B.C. programme*, my first thought was that it couldn't possibly be me! But it was, and if confirmation were needed, half the width of the front page read *Brum Boy's War Diary*, followed by its page number. Margaret suggested that this happening was sufficiently unusual to interest fellow members of B.P.L.'s [Birmingham Public Library] Association of former staff, hence this present contribution.

It is a fact that in 1940 4 members of BPL Staff – Ken Rider, Ken Boodson, Harry Sargeant and myself – were serving in France with the B.E.F. and experienced the 3 weeks German Blitzkrieg in May & early June that led to the B.E.F.'s retreat and final evacuation from Dunkirk. All four of us were wireless operators in A Section of the Territorial 48th Divisional Signals, based on Hall Green; and I must confess right away that I infringed military law by illegally keeping a very full diary from the time of our arrival in France in early January until our evacuation in late May/June. More a journal than a diary it formed the basis of my *Dunkirk Diary of a Very Young Soldier*, published (and launched over television) by BPL in 1989, to mark the 50th Anniversary of the outbreak of war and the Dunkirk Evacuation. The book was well received and before long was out of print.

About a year ago, settled into what I fondly imagined would continue to be a quiet retirement, I received, completely out of the blue, a phone call from the B.B.C., telling me of the major film series on Dunkirk that they were working on, and asking if I would be prepared to contribute to it. I agreed.

A novel feature of their programme was its Drama/Documentary form. The Drama element was to comprise 3 one hour programmes on successive evenings, presented by B.B.C. Television Channel 2. They were to portray real events and the people who carried them out; the latter of course being performed by Professional Actors. My own involvement was two-fold. First of all it seemed that the B.B.C. having come across my book in the course of wide ranging research and literature-searching, had found its general structure to be very appropriate to their own needs. Secondly, they had decided to use as a principal strand in the first two hours of their film, the activities and experiences, as described in my book, of the mobile wireless crew made up of three wireless operators – corporal Tich Humphreys, a very experienced 'old soldier' reservist in his mid 30's, my school friend Clive Tonry, and myself – both 19 year olds.

In addition to this Drama Component there was to be a supplementary interactive element, available to viewers with Digital Facilities. This was to give access to several of the well over 100 interviews carried out by the B.B.C. with surviving Dunkirk Veterans. Finally a separate hour-long film was to be devoted to interviews of a general 'overview' character, with a relatively small number of interviewees, of whom I was one.

My own experience of being interviewed I found both interesting and impressive. In deference, no doubt to the advanced age of most of us, the B.B.C. came to us, in our homes, rather than requiring us to travel to their studios. The interviewing for my own first session was carried out by the Script Editor, Lisa Osborne, and the script writer Neil Mckay, accompanied by considerable quantities of technical equipment. They selected our small sitting room as being best suited for their needs, removed or re-arranged various ornaments and items of furniture (all punctiliously replaced at the end), re-arranged the seating, amplified the lighting, and having seated me in my comfortable armchair, got down to work.

The script-writer handled the principal camera (which I subsequently learned cost £50,000!) while his partner's small but highly sophisticated camera was kept in continuous action (including some stills from my own albums). Questions were put to me by both of them, but in the second part of the session the script writer went through a very vigorous, virtually word by word survey of my diary entries for the relevant period. The whole session occupied 5½ hours. Very demanding for me, of course, but extremely impressive in its pursuit of absolute accuracy in the script team's own understanding and interpretation of the facts and events that I had experienced and recorded. What needs to be kept in mind, of course is that over 60 years had elapsed, and the staff involved in the interviewing sessions along similar lines to that first one, and of similar, c. 5½ hours duration.

After the conclusion of our interviews Clive Tonry and I maintained contact with the B.B.C. as their team moved on to the major task of cutting and editing their enormous accumulation of film and sound track. Actors were being selected to play the parts of the main cast; dates of presentation of the main drama began to firm up and were finalised at Feb. 18th – Feb. 21st and an invitation arrived from the B.B.C. to attend a previewing for cast and crew on the previous Sunday, Feb. 15th.

Around this time I began to experience an interesting phenomenon. Quite randomly and much to my surprise, phone calls began to arrive – from friends and relatives, neighbours, colleagues past and present. They began "I have just seen you on T.V.". The reason for this I soon realised was that the B.B.C. had embarked upon a quite substantial programme of 'trailers' for Dunkirk, which included brief glimpses of various cast members.

It must have been around this time too that I was living in a world that was somewhat surreal. Attendance at the Feb. 15th preview served to intensify this. There I was, at B.A.F.T.A. in Piccadilly, with my wife Joan and our younger son and his wife, waiting in an ante-room to its cinema before the films began, and being introduced not only to the Producer and Director, but also to a very promising young actor named Michael Legge, who was playing me, Wilf Saunders, in the films which were about to follow. This preview commenced with a brief introduction from Producer and Director and concluded with a brief appearance by Bert Evans, a survivor of the infamous Wormhout massacre, which unknown to us at the time, was taking place on May 28th, just down the road from the field where Clive and I were lying as temporary infantry, with rifles set at 300 yards. Bert was received by the preview audience with a standing ovation.

The presentation of the 3 one-hour films was quite a marathon, but a brief break between the second and third provided opportunity for a photograph with my own actor counter-part and likewise with Clive Tonry's, for passing on to Clive, who was unable to be present. Extremely enthusiastic applause from the audience of well over 200 followed the conclusion of each film and by the time the preview concluded it was clear that the wide-ranging and very complex design which the Producer and Director had planned and which to many of us seemed well nigh unattainable had been triumphantly achieved. We were not alone in this reaction. When the public release took place, during the following week, the tone from the critics was overwhelmingly one of praise and enthusiasm.

For me the influx of telephone calls and letters not only continued but increased after the broadcasting of the films, and with this arose a rather weird sensation of living in some sort of time-warp. One foot in the past, so to speak, with all these voices and events from my youth looming large: so much so that it would not have been too surprising if my parents and sisters had arrived on the scene!

All in all, a most enjoyable experience to carry with me as I resume that interrupted 'quiet retirement'.

Wilf Saunders, 2004

Appendix IV

PLACES IN ENGLAND

MENTIONED IN THE DIARY

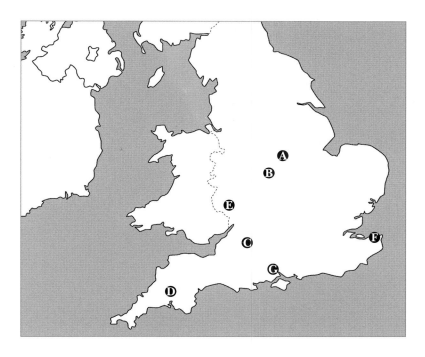

A. Alfreton   First regroup after Dunkirk.
B. Birmingham   Home & enlistment for Wilf Saunders.
C. Chilton Foliat Location of 'Fowl Pen' temporary billet.
D. Devonshire   Regroup location for 48th Division Signals.
E. Hereford   Regroup after Alfreton.
F. Margate   Return port after Dunkirk.
G. Southampton   Embarkation point for France 1940.

Appendix V

OBITUARY FOR WILFRED SAUNDERS CBE

Wilf with his wife Joan moved back to Sheffield in 1999 from Sawston, Cambridge to where he had first retired.

In July 2003 the B.B.C. got in contact with him to use the Diary (see letter). A small team of two B.B.C. Drama Dept Staff came to interview him and photograph him at home. He records that the two half day interviews totalled almost eleven hours, extracts of which were used by them for the Dunkirk Series.

At the end of January 2004 he was invited (see letter) to the Cast and Crew Showing of the completed Docudrama Dunkirk. To quote their letter "we really couldn't have done it without you!".

The Showing in London in mid February, a prelude to the Bafta Awards, went very successfully and Wilf was able to meet Michael Legge who played him in the T.V. Series along with the other actors who played his comrades. He was photographed with them in front of the B.B.C. Placard advertising the series which was a proud moment for him.

The series went out on three days at the end of February to much acclaim and to the surprise of many people who suddenly saw him appear on the screen in a 'Trailer' advertising the series. His daughter in law was startled to hear his voice behind her (from the T.V.) when she knew he was fifty miles away!

Until the end he retained a real interest in World War Two, building up a large library and revisiting the areas where he was stationed.

Sadly Wilf Saunders died in July 2007 after a short illness, aged 87. He is survived by his wife Joan and his two sons John and Peter and their families.

John M. Saunders – November 2009